D0125617

How to Help Yourself

HOW TO HELP YOURSELF

Robert J. Hastings

BROADMAN PRESS
Nashville, Tennessee

© Copyright 1981 ● Broadman Press
All rights reserved.

4252-83
ISBN: 0-8054-5283-4
Dewey Decimal Classification: 158
Subject headings: PSYCHOLOGY, APPLIED // CHRISTIAN LIFE

Library of Congress Catalog Card Number: 80-70917
Printed in the United States of America

"This is all that I have learned: God made us plain and simple, but we have made ourselves very complicated" (Eccl. 7:29, TEV).

"It is better to win control over yourself than over whole cities" (Prov. 16:32, TEV).

Contents

Prologue

It was the summer of 1930, and Herbert C. Hoover was in the White House. America was reeling from the first blows of the Great Depression.

I was a timid, barefoot boy of six, ready to enter first grade in the fall. I knew little about Herbert Hoover and high finance. But I had confidence in my uncle Bob Wollaver, who lived on a scrabbly farm, twelve miles south of Marion, Illinois.

Uncle Bob was a Democrat, living in a Republican stronghold. During the thirties, I often heard him say, "I wouldn't vote for no Republican if I was a-starvin' to death." To hear him tell it, Herbert Hoover brought the depression to Washington in his suitcase (we hadn't learned the word *luggage*).

On this particular evening, we were visiting my uncle Bob and his wife, Aunt Mattie. Like many farm families in those days, they pushed the dining table out on the screened back porch during hot weather. It was already dusk, the cows were milked, and Aunt Mattie brought a flickering kerosene lamp to the table. Since I was a town boy, a kerosene lamp was sort of eerie, especially when a hoot owl squalled from a nearby woods.

The meal was bountiful. Although cash was short in the thirties, Uncle Bob always had plenty of fresh milk; butter; country ham; thick, fat bacon; and garden vegetables. Aunt Mattie set the table with what looked to me like the abundance of the Garden of Eden.

Uncle Bob would roll up his sleeves and pass the fried chicken. As he did, he would say, "You know, folks, I just wish that Herbert Hoover and his wife could come down here to Johnson County just *one* time and eat like poor folks. If he could see what we have to live on, he'd do something about this depression."

Then he added, as always, to my parents, "Now Eldon, Ruby, and Bobby, you see what's set before you. Just reach and help yourself." And we did.

I've never forgotten what he said about the Hoovers coming to Johnson County. Believe it or not, I actually thought they might. On future visits, as Dad drove up the lane to my uncle's house, I always strained to see if there might be a big, black limousine parked out front. And I did so with apprehension: *What if the Hoovers did show up? Would I know what to say to them?*

Of course, the Hoovers never came; I was never forced to "find something to say" to the president of the United States.

But I've never forgotten Uncle Bob's invitation, still heard at many tables to this day, "Now help yourself!"

I've reached back into my boyhood and chosen "help yourself" as the theme of this book. It expresses an age-old truth: Each person can and must help himself if he can.

As a teenager, I read the sermon, "What to Do with Life's Burdens," by the late George W. Truett. It is in his book *A Quest for Souls.*[1] Truett first delivered the sermon in a revival sponsored by the Broadway and College Avenue Baptist churches of Fort Worth.

The simple sermon is based on three texts:

1. "For every man shall bear his own burden" (Gal. 6:5).

2. "Bear ye one another's burdens, and so fulfil the law of Christ" (Gal. 6:2).

3. "Cast thy burden upon the Lord, and he shall sustain thee" (Ps. 55:22).

Truett was not putting down the help that comes from God

and friends. He was simply saying that the very first question to ask in the face of a problem is, What can I do about it myself? Helping oneself is not all one can do, nor do one's own resources represent all the help you can get. But it's the place to start.

The problems that you and I can do something about are treated in this book. Henry W. Longfellow said, "If you would write, look within." That's what I've done. I've reviewed some of the crises in my own life and share how I faced them. In many instances, friends as well as my faith in God played major roles. But the emphasis is on how I helped myself.

Really, I shouldn't be writing a book like this. I've had no training in counseling; I never had a course in psychology. I have no credentials except experience, common sense, and a faith in the unlimited resources of heaven.

Also, I have no great "success" stories to tell. I've never been "delivered" from alcoholism or other drug abuse. I've never been in jail, never had a nervous breakdown, never consulted a psychiatrist (although there was a time when I would have benefited), never been divorced, never attempted suicide. I've never suffered a serious injury, never been in an automobile accident, and in my fifty-seven years have spent only six nights in a hospital (and that was only a precautionary measure).

My problems have been ordinary ones, and I've certainly been average in coping with them. But then, aren't most of us average?

So if you're a super saint or plagued with super problems, save yourself the trouble of reading what I have to say: I probably don't speak your language.

Today we are overwhelmed with "professional" problem solvers. Some of them tell us to grab the world by the tail and march out into the great arena of life and be a WINNER, to be Number One, and to excel—if necessary—by intimidation! And goodness knows, all of us want to win.

You've heard about TM, LSD, SMC, est, and ESP. Other self-help groups and religions or sects include Zen Buddhism, Hare Krishna, scientology, sorcery, black magic, witchcraft, astrology, palmistry, telepathy, the occult, Ouija boards, and nude encounter groups.

I think it's about time to help ourselves . . . to be ourselves, even if that's number two, number three, or whatever.

Caution: If, by the time this is published, I have walked in my sleep, fallen down the stairs, spent six weeks in the hospital with sixteen broken bones, declared backruptcy, become addicted to morphine, and then attempted suicide, use you own judgment about reading.

I don't mean that to sound flippant. And if it does, forgive me, for no one knows the hour when a crisis of unimagined proportion may come. I only say it to underscore my ordinariness and to dispel any grandiose ideas about my "expertness" in the common problems of life.

Note

1. George W. Truett, *A Quest for Souls* (Nashville: Broadman Press, 1917).

1
When You Wonder Whom to Trust

Sooner or later, our heroes let us down. No one is perfect, regardless of how much we idolize him. As adults, we find this idea relatively easy to handle. But as youngsters, it's harder. If, in our childhood, someone we love disappoints us in a moment of weakness, the injury is doubly hard to bear. At worst, it leads to lifelong bitterness and cynicism. At best, it only makes us suspicious.

How can we handle the shock of misplaced trust? It's better handled in advance of the shock. We can remind ourselves that the strongest suffer weaknesses, the purest wear stains, and the kindest show cruelties.

To enable you to help yourself at this point, I'm not listing a lot of "thusly" and "thatlys," guidelines and by-lines. Instead, I'm reaching back to my childhood, sharing a part of me and my family. If, in my experience, you discover a mirror in which you see just a little of yourself, perhaps you'll also find insights to help you cope with misplaced trust.

In the late afternoon of May 13, 1968, I pulled up at the Travelodge in Springfield, Illinois, where I had a reservation. As I started to register, the desk clerk asked, "Are you Mr. Hastings? A call just came for you. Your father died this morning."

I was not surprised, for my father had been critically ill. But I was surprised that no tears came to my eyes. In fact, I was almost embarrased that I showed so little grief in front of the clerk. But

13

Dad was eighty-six. The last time I had seen him he made no response. His frail body was curled up almost fetus-like, his arms and legs occasionally jerking, as if from some electrical shock deep in his muscles.

I notified David Williams, pastor of the Springfield Southern Baptist Church, where I was to speak that night. Then I got in my car and began the drive to Marion, Illinois, where Dad was to be buried.

During that four-hour drive into the gathering dusk and night, I reviewed Dad's impact on my life.

To be frank, Dad and I were not particularly close. I say "particularly" because there were some warm moments of closeness, which I will describe. But there were also gaps.

For one thing, Dad was considerably older than the fathers of most of my peers. Born in 1881, he was forty-three when I came along in 1924. Not that forty-three is old, but he reached his sixtieth birthday while I was in high school.

You can't always justify how adolescents react. They have certain feelings, even though they shouldn't. As a teenager, I saw Dad as an old man. (Strange how our ideas of *old* and *young* change as we age ourselves!). This really hit when I was in high school. We attended a father-son banquet sponsored by the Hi-Y club. I looked around and realized that Dad, with maybe one exception, was the oldest man in the room. The lines on the back of his neck stood out in marked contrast to the more youthful faces of the other fathers.

There was a gap in our interests. Dad had little formal education, finishing only the fifth grade in a one-room schoolhouse with seven- and eight-month terms. The school year was often interrupted by impassable roads in the winter.

By the time I was ten, I had gone to school more than Dad. Eventually I went to graduate school and earned a doctor's degree. Dad was always a slow reader, taking an hour or more to read a few stories of local interest in the Marion newspaper. He knew little of magazine articles, and I'm guessing he read less than a half-dozen books in his lifetime.

Yet, I never felt superior. I respected the experience and wisdom he had learned in daily life, which often exceeds the value of classroom studies. But still the gap was there. He was a man who made his living with his hands, growing up on a farm, then graduating to the coal mines as a youth.

Driving to Marion the night Dad died, I recalled three tender moments that brought a lump to my throat. Marion had been my home until I entered college. It's strange how we review our childhood. We pick out two or three bright moments, which, at the time, seemed trivial, but with the passing of the years, glow in our memory.

In September of 1930, I was in Grace MacDonald's first-grade class at the Jefferson School in Marion. She assigned us "The Gingerbread Boy," the first story in our first-grade reader.

I took my reader home that day. After supper, Dad was sitting in his favorite rocking chair behind the heating stove (although it was still too warm for a fire). I liked to stand at his side, on one of the rockers, and sway back and forth as he rocked. As I did so, he opened my reader to the first page and began to repeat slowly, "I am a gingerbread boy, I am, I am." Then he took my hand and guided by fingers slowly under the words as he repeated: "I am a gingerbread boy, I am, I am."

And then, as if a magic wand danced across the page, those words sprang to life before my eyes. I could see the gingerbread boy. I could see that words are expressed with tiny markings on pages, that everything has a name, and that if you know those names and words you can read just about anything in the world!

The excitement of that moment has never left me. Even now as I write these words, tears are brimming in my eyes, begging for a chance to spill down my cheeks.

Much of my life has been devoted to words, both verbal and written. Little of my father's life was devoted to words, at least in a formal setting. But he was the one who unlocked their magic to me.

As I drove on, through Vandalia and Centralia, I also remembered a spring morning when I was recovering from a minor illness. I guess I was four, maybe five. Mom had put me to bed in the front bedroom, which faced the east. We used it only in times of illness or for guests. Dad came in that morning and sat on the edge of my bed. The sun was streaming in the east window and just outside, spring birds were singing with all their might.

"Bobby," Dad said to me, "do you hear the birds singing? Do you know what they're saying? Why, they're singing, 'Bobby, get up! Bobby, get up!"

I listened, and sure enough, they were, and I was so amazed that they knew my name! I felt like jumping out of bed and bounding down the steps into the beauty of that spring morning. Most of all, I felt a magical closeness to my daddy, deep and warm and poignant.

As I neared Marion, another beautiful picture flashed before my mind. It was the afternoon of my ordination to the ministry. I was only eighteen. At that service, Dad put his arms around me and whispered something very dear into my ear. I can't tell you what he said until I describe another memory, not altogether pleasant. That picture is laced with both sunshine and clouds and goes back to my early boyhood. It was my first serious bout with misplaced trust.

When I was growing up, Dad had a drinking problem. Just how big the problem was, I don't know; children have the capacity both to exaggerate or to minimize what hurts them. So it may have been worse than I recall, or better.

I don't mean Dad was a drunkard or even a near-alcoholic. But his drinking was a problem, regardless. Few of our relatives or neighbors knew, for Mom made every effort to cover up for him. And most of the time, she was successful.

I know that with many people, drinking is socially acceptable, that it's been glamorized in song, literature, theater, and the like. Millions of American families serve alcoholic beverages in their homes; in some cultures, it is even more common. I've heard all the arguments for drinking in moderation and read all the advertisements that link drinking with sex appeal, sophistication, and the "good life." But I'm not impressed.

Say what you will, alcohol is a dangerous drug. Its victims lie strewn across the landscape of time—highway wrecks, prisons, divorce courts, mental institutions, welfare offices, and industrial accidents. Its carnage is indescribable; its cost, astronomical. Never has so much good been said about so much evil as in the praise of beverage alcohol.

Maybe I'm prejudiced because of the pain it brought to me as a boy. I cannot be forgiving of those who advertised, sold, and distributed beer and whiskey to my dad. Yet I don't want to be too judgmental. Maybe Dad did well to survive, for example, the Great Depression years when he so badly wanted to work. Maybe his few bouts with drinking helped to bridge an impossible situation. I don't know. I just know the pain.

As much as I admired Mom's stand against drinking, I often felt that maybe she went too far. If she had been less defensive, more tolerant, maybe the problem would have gone away. Again, I don't know. I just know the pain. She did what she thought was right.

Dad drank only occasionally, but when he did, it was to excess. He would come home late, often unable to undress, and sometimes vomiting into the night.

He enjoyed going to town on Saturday afternoons and visiting with his friends around the public square, a favorite gathering spot in Marion during the thirties. And as long as farmers still drove wagons to town to do their "trading," the old hitchrack just a block northeast of the square was also a favorite gathering place. Nearby were several taverns, and if you go to Marion today, some are still there.

I think Dad's problem was the influence of certain friends more than anything else. Looking through my boyhood diary, I find this poignant entry, dated July 19, 1937:

> Rained this morning and was cold. Dad went to town at noon and didn't get back until 7:00 PM. About 5:30, I went uptown and got policeman to look in saloons for him, but didn't find him. He had about $225 with him.

This was not long after the death of my brother, who left a small insurance policy. The $225 was evidently some of the proceeds which Dad had with him. All the banks in Marion closed during the thirties; whether one had reopened by 1937, I do not remember. However, many people were still suspicious of banks and hesitated to make deposits. Because of this extra money Dad was carrying, Mom was unusually concerned. That was a small fortune in 1937. Three days earlier, on July 16, I noted in the same diary that my headlight batteries on my bicycle were dead and that I didn't know when I would get any new ones, unless I got another yard to mow. That day, I had "mowed the Brown's yard for 50¢."

Mom was almost paranoid in her fear that a neighbor or relative might know when Dad was drinking. So on any given Saturday afternoon, if he failed to come home in time for supper, Mom feared the worst. Near dark, she closed the doors, and we would sit inside until bedtime, never turning on a light. If anyone knocked at the door, we didn't answer.

Such was more traumatic during the winter, with early dusk and long nights. Sitting in a darkened house for several hours, waiting for bedtime, with nothing to do but wait and listen for steps on the porch was traumatic for a boy who loved both his parents.

Finally I would go to bed, only to be awakened and listen to . . .

I'll never forget the last time this happened. I was in high school and about fourteen years old. By then we had a car. On that Saturday night, Dad missed the garage door, causing slight damage. When he came inside, his billfold was empty. He had no money. All of his identification was missing, including his Social Security card and driver's license. He couldn't remember where he had been or who might have rifled his billfold.

The next morning, Dad was able to come to the breakfast table, although his face was drawn and colorless. He ate in silence, his head down, looking neither to the right nor left. I was dressed for Sunday School, for Mom always insisted that I go on to church, carefully reminding me not to say anything about what happened the night before or why she was not in church herself. I became expert at saying nothing.

After Dad finished eating, he put his fork aside, drank a last swallow of coffee, then looked across the table at me.

"Son," he began, "you'll never see me again like you did last night."

Mom said nothing. I said nothing. I wanted to believe him, but I didn't. Yet there was a new firmness in his voice, a confidence, a resolution.

In a few minutes I picked up my Bible and Sunday School quarterly and walked out the door for the First Baptist Church downtown. I didn't believe Dad, yet I didn't disbelieve him. I decided just to wait and see.

So far as I know, Dad never touched another drop of liquor. A few Sundays later, he started to church, where he was already a member. Nothing else was ever said. But never again did we wait in a darkened house; never again did what little money we have go for an industry that traffics mercilessly in the minds and bodies and souls of its victims.

With that promise to me, Dad grew ten feet tall in my estimation. He showed me that a man can change, that a man can turn his life around. At that breakfast table, he taught me the greatest lesson of his life. Joy over that lesson brought the tears as I neared the outskirts of Marion, not the fact Dad's tired body was asleep for the last time. The lesson Dad taught me was: when you face a problem, look first to your own resources, your own will power, your own self-determination.

Now for the ordination. It was at the First Baptist Church in Marion on a Sunday afternoon in March, 1942, during my freshman year in college. I had been called to a little country church between Marion and Herrin called Crenshaw Crossing. The members there had requested my ordination.

At the close of the service, Pastor Noel M. Taylor invited me to stand at the front while everyone came by to shake hands. As Dad neared me, he broke down, put his arms around me, and whispered, "My son, my son . . ." I cannot describe our closeness, the pride I sensed in him. My mind raced back a few years to that breakfast table when he had also said, "My son." What he said at my ordination was just an outgrowth of what he had said then.

Yes, thank God, life is long enough to rebuild lost trust, and most folk are big enough to merit that trust if we look deep within them.

We buried Dad on May 15, two days before my forty-fourth birthday. But the day we buried him, I was still forty-three, his age when I was born.

Dad was a common man. He accumulated little wealth, received no formal honors, never had his picture in a newspaper.

But at a crossroads in my life, he made a promise; the courage of that promise still inspires me.

The bright, May morning when I went to the funeral home to take Dad's clothing, Mom included two pairs of his long union suits. "Tell Mr. Mitchell [the mortician] to put both pair on him," she said, "it will help to fill him out. He's so thin." I detected in her words the ageless wisdom of Proverbs 31:10,11, 21: "Who can find a virtuous woman? for her price is far above rubies. The heart of her husband doth safely trust in her. . . . She is not afraid of the snow for her household: for all her household are clothed with scarlet."

From the time Dad was fifty, with each new suit he'd say, "I guess I'll be buried in this." He missed several of his predictions! We finally selected a gray suit; the one, I recall, he wore at his fiftieth wedding anniversary in 1960. Mom said we ought to buy a new white shirt and tie to go with it.

I walked up to the public square to Albright's Men's Store, which during my boyhood went under the name, "Powell's Best Clothes in Egypt" (a motto painted on barn roofs all over southern Illinois).

They were having a late spring sale, and I found an all-cotton Manhattan dress shirt for half-price. How that would have pleased Dad, for seldom did he enjoy the luxury of a brand-name shirt such as Arrow or Manhattan. And I bought it at half-price too!

The birds were singing as I walked out North Market Street to the Mitchell Funeral Home, with Dad's two pair of long underwear under one arm and the new white shirt under the other.

I hope there'll always be birds to sing, fathers to herald their singing, boys to listen, and trust to rebuild.

2
When Your Body Lets You Down

Our physical bodies confine us, as well as liberate us. A strong body helps us do more, be more, and enjoy more. A sick or injured body may confine us to our home, our bed, or even a wheelchair.

What steps can we ordinary people take to keep our bodies well and strong? How can we compensate when illness or accident takes its toll?

To answer this, I'm going to be autobiographical, reaching into an incident in my boyhood. If you can identify with even a portion of my experience, you may gain some helpful insights.

It was April of 1938, and I was just a few days short of my fourteenth birthday and eighth-grade graduation. I hit puberty that spring about like a car going 70 MPH on an interstate highway when it hits an unexpected pothole. The bruise from that bump was about six years in healing. But by the time it did, I had come to appreciate the role that emotion plays in physical health.

Is There Life After High School? is a book by Ralph Keys. In this book, Keys quotes John A. Rice as saying, "A man may remember his childhood with pleasure, but where is one who does not wince at the memory of his adolescence?"[1]

My diary tells me that on Wednesday afternoon, April 14, 1938, I had stayed after school for band practice. Practice included marching because we were preparing for the state band contest in Bloomington, Illinois, on May 14.

On my way home from band practice, I stopped at the Modgellan residence near our home on North State Street to mow their lawn, using an old-fashioned push mower. The grass was tall; for April, it was a hot day. I stopped next at the Biggs residence to mow their yard, but only got half way through before the sun set.

"I was exhausted and was sick all night," I wrote in my diary, "couldn't sleep, vomited, had fever, etc."

On the surface, those fourteen words seem little more than an upset stomach. But there was more. The next morning, I started turning numb all over. My feet and hands were cold. I felt as if I were coming apart at the seams. I got panicky. My heart raced; I thought I might die. I trembled and my teeth chattered as if I were having a chill. The doctor came; I took some medicine and felt better. A few hours later, the numbness hit me again. I sensed the apprehension in my parents' eyes. I thought I was even sicker than I was.

For the next six years or so, I was haunted by the obsession that I might die unexpectedly, that something was wrong with me which no one could diagnose. Looking back, I realize it was probably an anxiety neurosis. Or, as Willard Gaylin puts it in his book, *Feelings,* I was a victim of somatization, which is the conversion of anxiety into physical symptoms.

Two years earlier, in April of 1936, my twenty-one-year-old brother, LaVerne, had died suddenly after a five-day illness. The diagnosis was diabetes. Death probably resulted from insulin shock (a death that could be prevented today).

I think my parents—especially my mother—went through such trauma over LaVerne's sudden death that, subconsciously, they determined that a similar illness would not slip up on me, their youngest. I don't say they intended to convey this fear to me, but children have a way of picking up nonverbal signals from their parents. I sensed it, whether I heard it in so many words.

Lest you condemn my parents for being oversolicitous, let

me add that this was before the day of antibiotics, vaccines, and the "miracle" drugs. Tuberculosis, diptheria, pneumonia, and the like were still "dread" diseases. Scarlet fever had been epidemic in Marion the previous winter. At Christmas, our vacation had been extended eighteen days in an effort to curb the spread of scarlet fever. Two of my boyhood friends had scarlet fever that winter, and both died the following summer of complications. I still remember the impact of their funerals on my impressionable mind. They were buried within five days of each other: Bruce Linck on Sunday, July 3, 1938, and Bobby Lowe on the following Thursday, July 7. *Maybe the next one will be another Bobby,* was the thought that wormed its way into my mind.

I suppose I had the normal amount of illness during high school—colds, flu, and one bout with streptococcus plus a kidney infection. But the slightest illness activated my fear that, like my brother, I might die suddenly with no one who really knew what was wrong with me and no one to help. Occasionally, the numbness and shivering, and especially "a nameless dread and fear," would reoccur.

My parents took me to a number of doctors during those years—though they did not constantly parade me into doctors' offices. Each time the diagnosis was the same, "I don't think there's really anything wrong with this boy."

The summer I was sixteen, as I recall, an incident occurred that should have helped me recognize my problem. But I didn't catch on. For several weeks that summer, I was bothered with depression. I didn't know it was called that, didn't even know that's what I had. I just know that in the mornings, I felt fine. But shortly after noon, as soon as you could tell the day had passed its zenith, the depression set in. And the nearer to sunset, the worse I felt.

One afternoon Mrs. H. O. Belford, who was my mother's

Sunday School teacher and whose husband was city superintendent of schools, came to visit.

Mrs. Belford was a large, jolly woman who shook all over
when she laughed, and she laughed most of the time. One eye
either didn't focus or was artificial; I never knew which. Anyway,
when she looked at you, you never knew if she was really looking
at you or past you. She didn't tell a lot of jokes, for she didn't have
to. Everything was funny to her.

By the time Mrs. Belford left, it was dark. Usually that was
the time I was feeling my lowest. But I felt great! "If Mrs. Belford
came every day, I'd never feel sad again," I told myself. Years
later I read Norman Cousins's book, *Anatomy of an Illness,* in
which he discusses the role of humor and a wholesome attitude
toward well-being.[2] Then I understood Mrs. Belford's secret. Her
secret is also found in Proverbs 17:22: "Being cheerful keeps you
healthy. It is slow death to be gloomy all the time" (TEV). But my
good feeling was short-lived.

Did I confide in anyone? Of course not. In the first place, I
didn't understand my feelings enough to verbalize them. As best I
remember, I'd never heard the words *psychiatrist* or *counseling,*
especially as related to adolescents. Oh, I'd heard about "crazy"
people and "lunatics," but all I knew was that something must be
physically wrong with me that no one could diagnose.

Psychoanalyst Theodore I. Rubin, MD, lists fifty warning signals that indicate a need for professional help. Two of them explain my struggles as a teenager: (1) An uncontrollable compulsion to perform certain acts or rituals without knowing why, and
(2) preoccupation with illness and death.

When I entered Southern Illinois University at Carbondale, I
felt compelled to earn my degree in three years. So starting with
the first semester, instead of taking the recommended fourteen to
sixteen hours, I signed up for about nineteen. By taking an over-

load each semester and going to summer schools, I graduated with honors two years and nine months after I enrolled as a freshman.

I don't say this with pride; for in my hurry, I missed so much. Why I had such a compulsion, I don't know. Perhaps I felt the whole world was out there waiting for me to save it!

I paid most of my college expenses and added to a savings account for seminary by holding two part-time campus jobs. Also, I served student pastorates on weekends. I felt no self-pity or sense of being a martyr. I liked it! I was elated at being able to attend college and hold two jobs at the same time, plus serving churches which needed help.

Getting away from home and being on my own during college helped free me from some of the death obsession of my high school years. I felt good and never missed a day of work, school, or a Sunday of preaching because of illness. Until the spring of 1944.

Exams week was over. I felt let down, emotionally and physically. That Friday night I went to bed early at the boys' rooming house where I lived at 313 West Grand in Carbondale. When my roommate, Alan Miller, came in around 11 PM, he casually mentioned that I didn't look well. We joked about it. Perphaps to relieve the post-exam tension, we decided to play a prank on other boys in the house.

Alan switched off most of the lights. I turned my face to the wall. When some of the fellows came in, Alan met them, serious faced. In a whisper, he told them I was "critically" ill. Subdued, they entered our room and fell for the act completely.

What happened next, I can't exactly describe, but some of the old fear came over me I'd known as a thirteen-year-old, on another spring night when I was near exhaustion. Suddenly, I *was* sick.

Before I knew what was happening, my roommates "helped"

me to a car and drove me to the Holden Hospital. It was well past midnight. Dr. Ben Fox checked me over and concluded that I had all the symptoms of appendicitis.

Right away, I should have said, "Look, Doctor, I'm just tired and nauseated; this is all a big joke. I don't have appendicitis any more than you do." But I didn't. I was too embarrassed.

Instead, I started screaming. I could see my parents, roused from bed by the telephone, rushing over to Carbondale, no doubt blaming themselves. Worst of all, I could see myself dying (needlessly) in surgery. By the time I quieted down, Dr. Fox said, to my everlasting relief, "I think we'll wait until morning." That was good enough news to make me sleep soundly all night.

E. M. Norman, a Baptist layman who befriended many college students through the years, came to see me the next morning. "I understand you kept them awake up here last night," he said in a kindly voice. I was too embarrassed to say anything. Anyway, the surgery was called off and in a day or two I was back in classes. I never did tell Dr. Fox the truth.

By that time I was engaged to Bessie Emling, whom I had met as a freshman. We planned to marry the next spring. I was haunted now by another fear—what if one of these death-obsession "spells" came on after we married? I couldn't stand the thought of telling this beautiful girl the "truth" about myself.

I decided once and for all to find what was really "wrong" with me. So I made an appointment at the Missouri Baptist Hospital in Saint Louis for a complete checkup, thinking that doctors who knew nothing about me or my past might give me a better diagnosis.

The following August, I entered Missouri Baptist for a couple of days. Looking back, I'm also chagrined by how I even got in the hospital. Since it was wartime and gasoline was rationed, my college friend, J. A. Hausser, and I decided to kill two birds with one stone. We would take our dates, Elizabeth Johnson and Bessie, for a day in Forest Park in Saint Louis, then see *Alice Blue Gown* that night at the Muni Opera. Finally, they would drop me off at the hospital, then return to Carbondale.

We had a great time, and it was only as I said good-night to them at the hospital door, did I realize how silly I had been in combining a date with a trip to the hospital! My chagrin was doubled when I later learned that due to a burned out fuse, the three of them spent the night in the car in East Saint Louis, waiting for daylight to drive home!

The receptionist greeted me, "It's a rather strange time to be checking in for a physical." I could have said I was a strange patient.

I went through the usual tests, under the supervision of Doctor W. S. Wiatt and a Doctor Martin. I had never seen them before and haven't since.

The morning I was to go home, Dr. Wiatt came into my room. He sat down and began his diagnosis. "We've checked you over thoroughly and can't really find . . ."

Yes, I'd heard that before, I thought.

But he continued, adding something new. "I notice from your records that you're studying for the ministry. Like all young preachers, you probably have a lot of altruism. You have big ideas about all the people you're going to help, how you'll change them and motivate them for this and that.

"That's all well and good," he continued. "But I hope you'll remember that people are human, and accept them as they are, rather than what you want them to be. You must start where they are. Now, Son, I don't really know what's wrong, but maybe you're trying too hard and that's why you're upset."

He wrote out a prescription and handed it to me. "Now this won't solve everything. It's just sort of a tonic to make you feel better. Get it filled if you want to, and take it as you like. It'll help you feel better; but as I said, it's not the solution."

With that, he was gone, and I got dressed. I walked out the front door and caught the Hodiamont streetcar to Union Station to catch the 2:20 PM Illinois Central for Carbondale.

As a boy growing up, I'd always thrilled at the sight of Union Station, located at Eighteenth and Market, one of Saint Louis's most prominent landmarks. At one time it had served 19 railroads, with as many as 250 trains a day coming and going.

Directly in front of Union Station was the Aloe Plaza, including the Milles Fountain. I stopped to watch the fourteen bronze figures amid the gushing fountains, themselves a symbol of the joining of the Missouri and Mississippi rivers at Saint Louis.

I enjoyed the ride back to Carbondale. The conductor called out the familiar towns, "Relay Station—East Saint Louis, Belleville, Freeburg, New Athens, Lenzburg, Marissa, Coulterville, Pinckneyville, Murphysboro . . . ."

I'd ridden this train many times, for a number of our relatives lived in Saint Louis. In fact, a few months before I was born, my mother and her oldest sister, Bertha Anderson, were making this trip to Saint Louis, when Mom, cupping a newspaper over her mouth for added privacy, leaned over and whispered, "Bertha, I'm in a family way."

And my aunt Bertha, in mock surprise, drew back and said, "Well, shut my mouth, Ruby! I thought you told me you were through havin' young'uns!"

Murphysboro was the last stop before Carbondale. Enroute, I'd been rehearsing Dr. Wiatt's words. They made sense in so many ways. They were simple words, but no one had ever explained life to me that way.

As the train pulled out of Murphysboro and crossed the Big Muddy River bridge, I slowly reached in my shirt pocket for the prescription. I folded it, then tore it in half. Then I folded it again, and once more tore it in half. I did this over and over, until it was shredded into tiny pieces, which I let flutter to the floor.

A sudden feeling of inner calm spread through my body, permeating every crevice of my mind. In that moment of insight, I "saw" that good health doesn't come from the corner drugstore but that how we look at life affects our well-being far more than vaccines or surgery or psychotherapy. The fear that first enslaved me when as a ten-year-old boy I stood watching my brother's body being lowered into his grave in Maplewood Cemetery in Marion, slowly released its grip on me.

I may have gone all around the world to make my point, but the truth is that our mental attitudes are the first step toward good health. That's a point where all of of us can help ourselves. I'm not against professional help, surgery, drugs, or any other phase of medical science. I believe in all of them! I'm just saying that running from doctor to doctor, constantly dosing ourselves with vitamins and drugs, and a neurotic preoccupation with "What's wrong with me?" is not the primary road to good health.

The night I wrote this chapter, I read an article in the *Chicago Tribune,* by Ronald Kotulak and Jon Van. "Almost every American has been overdoctored. His body has been cut, drugged, prodded, probed, wired, bled, or X-rayed—much of it unnecessarily," they claimed.

The article also quoted Philip R. Lee, MD, of the University of California—San Francisco: "Very often the first thing a patient wants is surgery. If he can't have that, he'd like a pill. If he can't have a pill, he at least wants a diet. The last thing a patient wants is for the doctor to do nothing."[3]

Looking back, I am everlastingly grateful that in the summer of 1944, I had the good fortune to consult a doctor who decided to *do nothing!*

Good health is the result of building blocks, which we erect ourselves, one on top of the other, starting with positive faith and thinking, topped by good nutrition, sanitation, exercise, adequate rest, sunlight, and clean air. What we do for ourselves in this respect is often far more important than what anyone else can do.

I referred earlier to Norman Cousins's book, *Anatomy of an Illness,* in which he warns that panic itself is one of the most dangerous multipliers of disease. Among other things, Dr. Wiatt freed me from panic.

Cousins writes:

There is no real separation between mind and body. Illness is always an interaction between both. It can begin in the mind and affect the body, or it can begin in the body and affect the mind, both of which are served by the same bloodstream.[4]

When Cousins visited Albert Schweitzer, the missionary doctor in Lambarene, Schweitzer told him, "Each patient carries his own doctor inside him. They [patients] come to us not knowing the truth. We are at our best when we give the doctor who resides within each patient a chance to go to work."[5]

Dr. Wiatt released the doctor within me, and in so doing, proved himself to be the ultimate doctor.

Notes

1. John A. Rice as quoted by Ralph Keys, *Is There Life After High School?* (New York: Warner Books, 1977), p.15.

2. Norman Cousins, *Anatomy of an Illness* (New York: Norton & Co., 1979).

3. Article by Ronald Kotulak and Jon Van, *Chicago Tribune,* October 5, 1980.

4. Cousins, p. 5.

5. Ibid.

3
When Today Has Lost Its Fizz

Edward Stainbrook, a nationally known authority on today's society, says that one of the two leading complaints heard by counselors is the feeling that life is meaningless. Stainbrook, who is professor emeritus of psychiatry at the University of Southern California, lists depression as the second complaint.

At one time or another, a feeling that life is meaningless hits all of us. And when it does, the fizz goes out of today. This is no new problem. The writer of Ecclesiastes, written centuries ago, complained, "It is useless, useless, said the Philosopher. Life is useless, all useless. You spend your life working, laboring, and what do you have to show for it?" (1:2-3, TEV).

This feeling of doom is also found in one of the oldest pieces of writing in existence, a clay tablet dug up from the ruins of Babylon: "Alas, alas, things are not what they used to be; children no longer obey their parents; everybody wants to write a book; and the signs are multiplying that the world is soon coming to an end."

An article in the October 10, 1857, issue of *Harper's* magazine read, "It is a gloomy moment in history. Not for many years has there been so much grave and deep apprehension, and never has the future seemed so incalculable as at this time."

So if life has lost its challenge and you feel there is no rhyme or reason to anything, you're not alone. This fear has gripped people from time immemorial.

If you find yourself in this rut, what can you do? As I said in the Prologue, I'm strictly a nonprofessional. If you have deep-seated feelings of depression and meaninglessness, this one chapter is not likely to solve your problem. But maybe you will find a few steps you can take to help yourself, a foundation or two on which you start to build.

In facing meaninglessness in my own life, putting time in its true perspective has been helpful. Time, after all, is the stuff that life's made of. And if we are to find meaning and purpose in life, we will find them within the confines of what we call *time*.

I tend to think of time in terms of a circle. This probably comes from the circular nature of clocks, watches, sundials, and the like. The big hand makes a complete circle once an hour, and the little hand once every twelve hours. The subtle suggestion is that as we use up this twelve hours, we can start all over. But that is an illusion.

Time is more like a plane or a straight line than a circle (I'm talking about a lifetime, not eternity or infinity).

At any point in life, we occupy only a pinpoint of time, which we call *now* or *the present*. Yet what we call the present is constantly slipping into the past, like grains of sand through an hourglass. And what we call *the future*, or *tomorrow*, is piece by piece, minute by minute, grain by grain, becoming now.

The expression, "point in time," has become a cliché since Watergate. The only "point" in time is what I'm experiencing now. You can truthfully say, "At this point in time I'm reading this sentence in this book," but that's as far as you can go.

Once they have passed, "present" experiences intermingle, like raindrops which fall into the Pacific Ocean. Each "point" loses its identity. Likewise, there's no such thing as a "point in time" in the future, for there is no predictable future. To say there is a "point in time" in the future is like saying you can pinpoint one raindrop that will fall in the ocean during tomorrow's rainstorm.

Human life, partly due to its brevity, is constantly moving forward on a flat plane, not in a circle.

It's impossible to step in the same river twice because where we once stepped is now occupied by different water. Likewise, we cannot "step" into time at various "points." We stepped yesterday; we may step tomorrow. But the only reality is the step we're taking now, the sentence we're now reading, the extraneous sound we now hear, the feeling of warmth or cold we now sense on our bodies, the emotion of excitement or boredom that permeates us now.

In our search for meaning, let's imagine time as a flat plane, extending from left to right, and ourselves as a figure on that plane. We are moving slowly but persistently to the right. All to the left is past. All to the right is future. Only the point we occupy is here and now. But how we relate to the past, the present, and the future bears on our sense of meaning in life. Let's examine life under the common terminology of yesterday, today, and tomorrow.

Yesterday

I find that sifting out the bits and pieces of the past help me find meaning in the present. This was especially true after the death of my parents, in 1968 and 1970. Looking through old letters, Christmas cards, yellowed newspaper clippings, family photographs, and school certificates spread a warm feeling through me. Yet it was more than a nostalgia trip. It was truly going home again, if only in imagination, and rediscovering the values that molded my life.

I started putting those memories down on paper. In 1972, my most popular book, *A Nickel's Worth of Skim Milk,* was published.[1] Although I intended it as a memoir for family and friends, I discovered other readers were interested because it helped them to relive the Great Depression and what it was like to grow up in the thirties. Let me give one example.

Shortly after the book was published, I was teaching in a weekend workshop at McKendree College in Lebanon, Illinois. A woman, in her late seventies, using a walker, made her way with difficulty up the steps and to the registration desk.

"Why in the world do you think a woman in my condition is coming to a writers' workshop?" she greeted me, a twinkle in her eye. Then she explained her purpose was to meet me and thank me for my book.

"You see," she explained, "I'd just had a stroke and was lying helpless in a hospital bed. Moreover, I was hopeless inside, deeply depressed. I'd just given up my lovely home to move into government housing for the elderly, which I didn't like.

"So I just lay there, day after day, not responding. Then a friend gave me your book. As I read it, I broke out laughing, then crying, then laughing. A nurse, alarmed, called my doctor and told him I was going crazy! He advised her to leave me alone, that it was good for me to express my emotions, that I'd been keeping myself all penned up inside.

"What's more, it brought back so many fond memories of my childhood, parents, and their sacrifices. As I recalled how they had suffered and yet overcame, I decided there was hope for me. I, too, could cope with the problems of today. Immediately I started getting better. And that's why I'm here!"

We sometimes criticize older people for "living in the past." But just as it is claimed a drowning person's entire life passes before him in review, so the aged see value in sorting out the past. On summer evenings, long after the sun is set, we enjoy the afterglow, reflecting on the good time we've enjoyed or evaluating our mistakes so we can correct them tomorrow.

Dr. Elisabeth Kubler-Ross tells how dying patients also do this. "What they tell you are very tiny, almost insignificant moments in their lives . . . that they have long forgotten and they suddenly have a smile on their faces. And they begin to reminisce about little memories that make their whole lives meaningful and worthwhile."[2]

Since childhood experiences are indelibly written into our memories, it is not strange that we recall them, even though we may forget the name of a person we only met yesterday.

However, let me sound a warning. A morbid preoccupation with the past is dangerous. Telling ourselves that only the "good old days" were good and seeing no meaning in today inevitably leads to depression.

Memory plays a funny trick on us. The trick is that time tends to smooth out the rough edges of yesterday. We often savor life more in retrospect than as we go along. Thus, yesterday appears better than it actually was!

Were this not true, life would become unbearable as we age. If time did not remove the rough spots, the yearly accumulation of sorrow, disappointment, hurts, and the like would crush us.

Suppose you never got over a headache, the pain from each headache being added to the pain of the last one. You couldn't stand it! Neither could we bear an accumulation of emotional pain. We *must* see some of yesterday as the "good old days."

In his book *A Time for Being Human,* Eugene Kennedy warns of living too much in the past. He calls it an "elaborate fiction," for really, we are not there. We are in the present, like it or not. Preoccupation with yesterday can be a cop-out. "Nostalgia may be fun," he observes, "but living in the glow of shallow reminiscences . . . is bound in the long run to prove disappointing and undernourishing."[3]

When he was a boy, Joseph Egan climbed a bluff near La Crosse, Wisconsin, and carved his initials on a rock. Years later, in the summer of 1978, when he was fifty-one, Egan climbed that same bluff to revisit his initials. Losing his footing, he slipped and fell thirty feet to his death. Egan, a hospital chaplain, had with him some altar boys. It's believed he was attempting to show them this souvenir from his own boyhood.

There's nothing wrong in revisiting the scenes of one's childhood. This was a freak accident from which we dare not try to draw a "lesson." However, it suggests a basic principle in life: There is danger in being so preoccupied with yesterday that we live in the past. Christopher Morley spoke to this theme when he wrote: "Time is a flowing river. Happy those who allow themselves to be carried, unresisting with the current. They float through easy days. They live, unquestioning, in the moment."

All cars and trucks have big windshields, plus one or more rearview mirrors. This is a parable of life. Most of our attention should be focused on today's traffic, on what's happening right now. Or, as Morley said, "the moment."

Yet a safe driver frequently checks his rearview mirror so he knows what's coming up on him. Likewise, we study the past and profit from it because it continually has a bearing on today. But we don't dwell on the past, lest, like a driver who focuses constantly on the mirror, we drive blindly into tomorrow.

Another danger about the past is what bad memories might do to us. Take guilt. If we feed too much on our faults, they may trap us in a web of destructive guilt. After we've sought forgiveness, some closet doors should stay closed for good.

The same is true about past failures. If we dwell on these, their memory will discourage us from our best today. In his book *The Little Minister,* James M. Barrie noted, "The life of every man is a diary in which he means to write one story and writes another; and his humblest hour is when he compares the volume as it is with what he hoped to make it." Because of the humbling effect of comparing deeds with dreams, let's not linger too long on those pages of our memory books.

In summary, life will have more meaning today if we rightly draw inspiration from the best of our memories, but refuse to be overwhelmed by yesterday's bad marks.

Tomorrow

In my own search for meaning, I must admit I've had some problems with yesterday, especially when I wrote my boyhood memoirs. Fascinated by the rediscovery of my boyhood diary, I found myself thinking that maybe the best was over. So I had to have a little talk with myself.

But I've had more problems with tomorrow than yesterday when trying to find meaning in life. The future has always fascinated me. I guess I'm one of those obsessives who get upset if things don't move on schedule. I tend to identify with what psychology calls the *zeigarnik effect,* the urge to achieve, to finish things, to leave nothing hanging or dangling loose, to tie up everything in neat little packages.

If they are not careful, compulsive people will outdo God in anticipating tomorrow. A runaway imagination, coupled with the ability to anticipate tomorrow, can be a deadly combination. Dr. Daniel A. Sugarman, a psychotherapist at Saint Joseph's Hospital in Paterson, New Jersey, warns that the worst fears are invariably of the "what would happen if" variety. He calls this the "suppose" syndrome—suppose I fail a test, fall ill, lose my friends, or whatever.

Some of my compulsiveness came from my family. Dad often said, "I tell you, it just kills me to sit around with nothing to do." And if there'd been a long day of just sitting around the house, say entertaining company, by nightfall Dad would set out for a long walk. The Great Depression got to him not only because money was short but also because there were so few jobs to work at, so little to challenge.

I remember my uncle Bob Wollaver's energy. On his farm in southern Illinois, he would often hitch his plowing horses long before sunrise. Then he'd stand in place at the edge of his fields, waiting for enough light to plow a straight furrow.

I remember my aunt Bertha Anderson. I often stayed nights with her one winter during high school when my uncle was working as a night watchman.

At bedtime, Aunt Bertha put newspapers and kindling in her big, black cookstove, so it would be ready to light the next morning. She lived close enough to the town square to hear the courthouse clock. When it struck six, she bounded out of bed, ran to the kitchen, doused the kindling with kerosene, then struck a match. While she dressed, the fire roared up the stovepipe and in minutes, the big oven was ready for a pan of her homemade biscuits.

In no time, she had breakfast ready. On some cold mornings, the oven seemed to cook the biscuits before the fire warmed the room. I sat at the table shivering—but not too cold to enjoy her homemade bread.

I think an early vocational choice also made me more conscious of the future. At the age of fourteen I felt that God was calling me to the ministry. So I geared up early for tomorrow! In fact, on my first date with Bessie Emling, I asked if she'd ever considered going on to a seminary after college. Since she said she had, I continued to date and later married her. We went to the seminary together!

Looking back, I often feel I grew up too quickly, that I became an adult too early. Erik Erickson says that persons, especially adolescents, need a "psychological moratorium" from the demands of life before they make the great decisions of life.

The mother of Carl Sandburg is credited with saying, "Life is short, if the early years are lost." The little fellow in second grade must have sensed this, when, one October day, his teacher asked what he wanted to be when he grew up. "I don't know," he replied, apologetically. "I don't even know what I want to be for Halloween!"

I've tried to resolve this conflict of living today and planning for tomorrow by accepting my compulsiveness. Yet I constantly whisper "that in this world fast runners do not always win the races, and the brave do not always win the battles" (Eccl. 9:11, TEV). However, there is great value in "tomorrowness," for "where there is no vision, the people perish" (Prov. 29:18).

Mr. Febble Mind's words in *The Pilgrim's Progress* thrill me, "But this I am resolved on: to run when I can, to go when I cannot run, and to creep when I cannot go. . . . My mind is beyond the river that hath no bridge." And the words of a track coach, talking to the boys on his pole vault team, are also encouraging: "Throw your heart over the bar, and your feet will follow."

Robert Goddard, a physics professor, wrote a paper in 1919 speculating on flights to the moon. Then in 1926, he launched the world's first liquid-fuel rocket. Although the rocket rose only 184 feet, Goddard's research paved the way for man's subsequent flight to the moon.

Where did Goddard get his inspiration? Not from preoccupation with today or nostalgia for the past. It came in a vision of tomorrow. He wrote about his vision of the future in his diary. This is an exerpt from an entry made when he was about seventeen years of age:

On the afternoon of October 19, 1899, I climbed a tall cherry tree at the back of the barn and started to trim dead limbs. It was one of the quiet, colorful afternoons of sheer beauty which we have in New England and as I looked toward the fields . . . I imagined how wonderful it would be to make some device which had even the possibility of ascending to Mars. . . . I was a different boy when I descended the tree.[4]

All of us can't be Robert Goddards. But each of us can climb a cherry tree now and then. Instead of trimming dead limbs from the past, we can look for brighter tomorrows. And in so doing, we will find more meaning for today.

Today

The ultimate meaning of life lies in what I do about today. Healthy attitudes toward yesterday and tomorrow will help, but they can't substitute for what I do now in this one "point in time" which is truly mine.

"Mrs. King had no control over the two dates which will be engraved on her tomb, 1904-1974. But she did influence that little dash in between the years." The speaker was the Reverend Otis Moss of Lockland, Ohio. He was emphasizing that what matters is what we do with our lives during the living. The occasion was the funeral for Mrs. Martin Luther King, Sr., in July of 1974. She had died at the organ in the Ebenezer Baptist Church in Atlanta, Georgia. She was playing "The Lord's Prayer" when an assassin's bullet killed her.

During the early days of World War II, two close friends were imprisoned by the Japanese in Singapore. One of the men, whose name was Jim, was placed in solitary confinement. His friend John desperately wanted to see him, but there was no way.

That is, there was no way until John hit on an ingenious plan. He started, in a rather amateurish way, to cut the hair of fellow prisoners. In fact, he grew so skillful that the Japanese appointed him as barber for those in solitary. This was exactly what John wanted. Once a month he visited Jim in solitary and cut his hair. But there was a catch. John could take nothing to the men in solitary. And he could say nothing to them of a personal nature.

However, John did get by with saying, "Now Jim, keep your chin up . . . keep your chin up . . . chin up now . . . chin up!" The guards, thinking these words had something to do with barbering, let him alone. Although he couldn't use the exact words, John's words meant, "Stop longing for yesterday; stop worrying about tomorrow; keep your chin up today."

Bernard Baruch celebrated his ninety-fourth birthday in August of 1964. A reporter asked Baruch to name the greatest person of his generation. He replied, "The fellow who does his job every day." He went on to say this might be a mother who dresses, feeds, and sends her children off to school each morning or a man who sweeps the streets.

One of the best-known prayers of all time includes only twenty-five words. Yet it has been quoted and reprinted millions of times because it speaks to the present. It's the official prayer of Alcoholics Anonymous and is commonly called the "Serenity Prayer."

Reinhold Niebuhr, a Protestant theologian, wrote the prayer in 1934 to conclude a sermon in a church in Heath, Massachusetts, where he was guest minister. After the service, a worshiper asked for a copy. Niebuhr, unaware of its future popularity, gave him the original, commenting, "Take this; I won't be needing it anymore." The prayer goes like this: "God, grant me the serenity to accept the things I cannot change; courage to change those things I can; and wisdom to know the difference."

Henry Ward Beecher said, "God asks no man whether he will accept life. This is not the choice. You must take it. The only choice is how."

The late Supreme Court Justice William O. Douglas was visiting his father shortly before he was to undergo surgery that proved fatal. The father told his famous son, "If I die, it will be glory; if I live, it will be grace."

Each in his own way—Baruch, Niebuhr, Beecher, and Douglas—said that what counts is what we do today. This is the meaning of Charles Kingsley's advice, "Thank God every morning when you get up that you have something to do that day which must be done, whether you like it or not."

J. B. Phillips, a British clergyman, is best known for his translation of *The New Testament in Modern English.* Back in the thirties, Phillips had a vivid vision of the hereafter during a serious illness. Phillips had this close encounter with death long before similar stories have appeared in print. He tells about it in his book, *365 Meditations for Today.*

Exhausted after surgery and unable even to move a finger, he overheard his doctor say, "I'm afraid he won't live till the morning." Then Phillips had this vivid dream. He was walking down a hill alone. He was depressed. All around him were ruined houses, pools of stagnant water, cast-off shoes, rusty tin cans, worn-out tires, and rubbish of every kind.

Across a little valley in the distance, he saw a beautiful vista of mountain and stream, field and forest, cloud and sky that made him gasp for breath. He started running toward this glorious world. Only a tiny stream separated him from the beautiful world. Then a figure in white appeared. He was gentle but authoritative. He smiled at Phillips, shook his head, and pointed him back to the miserable slope down which he had so eagerly run.

Deeply disappointed, Phillips burst into tears, awaking himself from the dream. The nurse asked, "Why are you crying? You've come through the night—you're going to live!"[5]

There are times when all of us would like to cross "the little valley and climb a beautiful vista of mountain and stream." Or we would like to return to the quaint paths of yesterday, bathed in a soft glow of nostalgia.

But meaning in life is finding significance in what is before us today, grateful for whatever good the past has given, hopeful for whatever good the future will bring.

All of us can profit from serendipity, "letting things happen." One must never preprogram and prepackage with such zeal that the spontaneous happenings never occur.

While thinking along these lines, I wrote the following column.

The Station

Tucked away in our subconscious minds is an idyllic vision. We see ourselves on a long, long trip that almost spans the continent. We're traveling by passenger train on nearby highways, of children waving at a crossing, of cattle grazing on a distant hillside, of smoke pouring from a power plant, of row upon row of corn and wheat, of flatlands and valleys, of mountains and rolling hillsides, of city skylines and village halls, of biting winter and blazing summer, and cavorting spring and docile fall.

But uppermost in our minds is our destination. A certain day and a certain hour and we'll pull in the station with bands playing and flags waving. And once we get there, so many wonderful dreams will come true, and so many wishes fulfilled, and so many pieces of our lives finally and neatly fitted together like a completed jigsaw puzzle. How restlessly we pace the aisles, damming the minutes for loitering . . . waiting, waiting, waiting for the station.

However, sooner or later we must realize there's no one station, no one place to arrive once and for all. The true joy of life is the trip. The station is only a dream. It constantly outdistances us. "When we reach the station, that will be it!" we cry. Translated, this means, "When I'm eighteen, that will be it! When I buy a new 450 SL Mercedes Benz, that will be it! When I put the last kid through college, that'll be it! When I've paid off the mortgage, that'll be it! When I win a promotion, that'll be it! When I have a nest egg for retirement, that'll be it! And I'll live happily ever after!"

Unfortunately, once we get "it," then "it" disappears. The station somehow hides itself at the end of an endless track.

"Relish the moment" is a good motto, especially when coupled with Psalm 118:24, "This is the day which the Lord hath made; we will rejoice and be glad in it." It isn't the burdens of today that drive men mad. Rather, it is regret over yesterday or fear of tomorrow. Regret and fear are twin thieves who would rob us of today.

So stop pacing the aisles and counting the miles. Instead, climb more mountains, eat more ice cream, go barefooted oftener, swim more rivers, watch more sunsets, laugh more, and cry less. Life must be lived as we go along. The station will come soon enough.[6]

Notes

1. Robert J. Hastings, *A Nickel's Worth of Skim Milk* (Carbondale, Ill.: University Graphics, Southern Illinois University, 1972).

2. Elisabeth Kubler-Ross as quoted by Eugene Kennedy, *A Time for Being Human* (Chicago: The Thomas More Association, 1977), p. 179.

3. Kennedy, p. 21.

4. Robert Goddard as quoted by R. A. Foster, "Vindication of Robert Goddard," *Coronet,* April, 1961, p. 118.

5. J. B. Phillips, *365 Meditations for Today* (Waco: Word Books, Publisher, 1974), pp. 32-33.

6. Robert J. Hastings, "The Station," *The Illinois Baptist,* January 2, 1980, p. 4.

4
When Your Halo Starts to Fade

For years, I've taken a grain of thyroid hormone each morning for an underactive thyroid gland. If one's thyroid gland is underactive, that means too little thyroxine is released into the blood stream, tending to make a person sluggish. If a thyroid gland is too active, the person may be extremely nervous. When thyroid glands are normal, people are unaware of the glands. Only when the gland under or overreacts does trouble set in.

The ego is that way. A normal ego makes it easier to keep our emotions in balance. But trouble results if one's ego is either under- or overactive.

The ego is what I consciously am. It's my personality, my individuality, my uniqueness. The ego is the real me, my completeness, including both my body and my personality or spirit. My ego is what I think of myself. It's how I conceive myself to be. It's a mental photograph of me.

An overactive ego results in egotism. Most of us don't like egotists. I know I don't. One reason may be that we tend to condemn in others what we fear in ourselves! The egotist seizes every chance to call attention to himself. He monopolizes the conversation, bragging constantly about his wife, his mother, his job, his boat, his car, his this and that. When you've heard one of his conversations, you've heard them all.

Egotism suggests self-worship, self-admiration, self-love, self-seeking, self-interest, and arrogance. It also suggests haughtiness, pride, vanity, conceit, insolence, and presumption.

Proverbs 17:27 says, "Someone who is sure of himself does not talk all the time" (TEV). And Proverbs 21:24 reads, "Show me a conceited person and I will show you someone who is arrogant, proud, and inconsiderate" (TEV).

I often think that some egotists are not egotists at all. They are merely playacting. That is, they are basically insecure and defensive people. To make up for a low self-esteem, they constantly brag about themselves.

But not all egotists are insecure. Some really believe all they say about themselves! Persons with strong egos often "succeed" in life by worldly standards. To me, success is more than big money, fancy titles, and national prominence. One might "succeed" in all of these, yet fail in the quality of his life, as related to family, friends, good health, personal satisfaction, and the like.

The underactive ego has its problems too. Just as we're turned off by the overbearing egotist, so we draw back at the timid, mousy wallflower who is so bashful and reticent that he would rather look down at the floor. He can't even look another person in the eye, let alone look up at the stars.

Such a person is at a distinct disadvantage. He barely has enough self-confidence to get out of bed in the morning. Like a cowed dog with his tail between his legs, the shy person slinks through life a loser because he sees himself as a loser to begin with. He allows others to wipe their feet on him because he perceives himself as a doormat and feels that is the only role he can play. He never wins because he never sees himself as a winner.

In extreme cases, this person may think of himself as undeserving even to live and thus may take his own life. But these are the exceptions. Most people with low egos just plod along, filling a niche, finding security in life's ruts.

Our egos are somewhat like halos. Some of our halos are so shiny and polished that they dazzle and blind those around us. We repel others with our jazziness. Happily, some halos enjoy a brightness that is normal and healthy. Still others are so dim as to be almost nonexistent.

In studying my own emotions, I have noticed that I am easily depressed if my ego is hurt. This is normal. The desire for recognition is one of the deep-seated drives of life. If that need is unmet, depression is likely. Studies show that the size of a paycheck cannot make up for a show of appreciation. Job satisfaction depends on how our employers treat us, as well as what they pay us.

This is true in all of life, not just on the job. If relatives or neighbors appreciate what we do for them, we are motivated to do even more. But if they give us the cold shoulder and rebuff us, low self-esteem followed by depression sets in. They've tarnished our halo. And as it fades before us, we feel sorrier and sorrier for ourselves.

"I'm always getting knocked off the Christmas tree" was a comment my mother often said when disappointed. "I feel like a cone without the ice cream, a human without a heart," is how one teenager described herself in her diary. Both statements may be exaggerations. Yet those feelings attack us during dark periods when we are haunted by negative feelings about ourselves.

How can we help ourselves when our egos grow raw and tender, when we are smothered in self-pity, when we conclude we are nothings and nobodies?

All I can do is share what has helped me. Each of my suggestions is something you can do for yourself, right where you are, right now.

1. *Refuse to practice amateur psychiatry!* Beware of the paralysis of analysis. Few people are more obnoxious than those who constantly probe themselves, asking why this happened or why they're this way and not that way. Ecclesiastes 7:29 notes, "This is all that I have learned: God made us plain and simple, but we have made ourselves very complicated" (TEV).

Primping in front of a mirror, hours on end, won't make you into a beauty queen. Likewise, endless hours of introspection will do little to polish the faded halo of self-esteem.

In an interview, Billy Graham told of a top psychiatrist, himself a Christian, who believes that some of our greatest problems are people who are self-analyzing themselves. "My son-in-law is a psychologist," Graham said, "and he said exactly the same thing. To try to analyze why one did this or that, he said, drives some people almost insane. And I've never been that type of self-analyzer. I've known people who have destroyed their Christian usefulness by this self-analyzation."

2. *Distinguish between vanity and a sincere desire to be a person of worth.*

Some well-meaning Christians have been known to pray, "Oh, to be nothing!" And all my life, I've heard that I'm to put God first, others second, and self last.

Humility is certainly a virtue in the Christian life.

Unless properly understood, such advice can lead us to think that any effort to be somebody is vanity. The inference is that only the nobodies are godly. Is it any wonder, then, that when our ego cries out for recognition, we feel guilty for harboring such a desire, as if it were some kind of base and lustful ambition?

A reasonable wish to be of worth is not a sin. When Jesus said, "Blessed are the meek" (Matt. 5:5), he was not complimenting shy, frightened, and cowardly folk. The Greek word for meek, *praos,* was often used to describe wild animals which had been tamed or broken. A tamed horse is not weak; rather, it is an animal whose cunning and power have been channeled into usefulness. So Jesus was praising those who are tempered, not those who are "nothing."

On the other hand, pride and raw ambition for selfish goals are wrong. On June 21, 1974, Charles W. Colson, former special counsel to former president Richard M. Nixon, was sentenced to one to three years in prison for obstruction of justice in the case of Daniel Ellsberg. Colson, one of the Watergate defendants, was sometimes called the White House hatchet man. A brilliant lawyer, blind in his loyalty, Colson was the kind of fellow who went for the jugular veins of his enemies.

But all that changed the day he saw himself in the pages of *Mere Christianity* by C. S. Lewis.[1] Colson was reading the part where Lewis said the greatest fault in human nature is pride. Pride, Lewis said, means we get pleasure not in just being rich, but in being richer than others; not just being nice looking, but nicer looking. Pride makes one feel superior. Since a proud person spends all his time looking down on someone else, he never sees anything above.

Lewis's book caused Colson to see himself as a victim of a pride that blinded him to anything higher and nobler in life. Not long after reading *Mere Christianity*, Colson surrendered his life to Christ.

If my life is ruled by raw ambition, then a hurt ego—or fading halo—will always pain me deeply. But if the goal is to be a person of worth, a temporarily fading halo will be no real problem. Our minds should center more on what we can mean to the world, rather than what the world can contribute to us.

This insight hit me with force when I was about twenty-six years old. I had just earned a doctor's degree from Southwestern Baptist Theological Seminary in Fort Worth, Texas, and the University Baptist Church in Carbondale, Illinois, had called me as pastor. Like all new pastors fresh out of the seminary, one of my first steps was to order stationery.

I was proud of that degree, for I had worked hard. Writing my thesis at the same time I was completing my classwork and also serving a student pastorate on weekends kept me more than busy.

I wanted to let people know I had a doctor's degree, but I wanted to do it with discretion. So I ordered two reams of stationery. On one ream I ordered the imprint "Dr. Robert Hastings"; on the other, just "Robert Hastings."

Although I am chagrined to admit this, I planned to use the stationery with *Dr.* when writing certain persons I wished to impress. For general church use, I planned to use the plainer stationery.

This bothered my conscience; and as I recall, I eventually used most of the *Dr.* stationery for scrap paper. I did so after asking myself, Did you earn a degree to increase your usefulness or to give you a bigger halo? Once I resolved that question, I could chuck the *Dr.* stationery.

I don't want to leave the impression that I'm a master of pride or the epitome of humility. I do mean to emphasize that if our lives are governed by ambition for selfish goals then the pain is always greater whenever our halos fade. But if our aims are to invest our lives for good, whatever the rewards, wounded egos heal easier, for we see, in effect, that egos are not all that important.

For fourteen years, I've edited *The Illinois Baptist,* a weekly newspaper. In this job, I've learned how fragile the human ego can be. How quickly a person is hurt if he gets less space than he thinks he deserves, if his picture isn't used, if his name is misspelled, or if the headline isn't big or prominent enough!

In communication workshops, I emphasize the difference between news and publicity. Publicity is what a person wants to see in the newspaper about himself; news is what the reader wants to see.

Vain persons look only for publicity. Others, seeking to be persons of worth and usefulness, are pleased if the good news about themselves is shared, but they're not crushed when overlooked or buried on the back page.

3. *Regardless of how badly you feel in your worst moments, remind yourself that, given time, you can make a worthwhile contribution.*

Buckminster Fuller, one of the world's most creative thinkers, has thirty doctor's degrees although he was kicked out of Harvard University and never finished college. He is best noted for conceiving the geodesic dome, which provides maximum strength and size with economy of materials. Yet one day as a youth, walking on the shores of Lake Michigan, he thought of himself as a failure and considered suicide. Then he concluded that he had no right to destroy himself, that his life contained some good.

Soviet dissident Aleksandr Solzhenitsyn had a similar, although more dramatic, experience. When visiting US Senator Jesse Helms in Washington, D.C., in 1973, Solzhenitsyn described how he had sunk into depths of despair while in a Soviet prison, unable for a long time to contact his family or friends.

One day during a ten-minute break, he decided the only way out was suicide. The easiest method would be to pretend to escape, knowing he would be gunned down before he had gone more than a few yards.

As he was getting to his feet to make such a break, a new prisoner who had just joined his work gang looked at him. Then, without a word, the new prisoner drew a cross on the ground. "I realized then," said Solzhenitsyn, "this was a sign from God that I was not to take my life."

When he returned to camp that night, he was told he would be released. Thus he was able to begin his work of documenting the horrors of Soviet life. Had he given in to his despair, the world would never know his great genius as an author.

4. *When your ego's hurting, don't make it worse by taking an inventory of "wrongs."*

First Corinthians 13:5 says, "Love does not keep a record of wrongs" (TEV). The American people keep records of nearly everything—births, marriages, property transfers, car titles, Social Security numbers, military service, educational degrees, deaths, and the like.

But don't clutter your mind with memories of hurts, slights, and offenses. If you do, they'll sting like fire when rubbed into the raw wounds of a hurting ego.

When Louis Evans, Sr., was pastor of the Hollywood Presbyterian Church in Hollywood, California, he sat one morning at his study window, watching some children at play. One of the children had found a dead bird. The children decided not only to bury the bird but also to conduct a "funeral." So one boy made a casket from a matchbox while another whittled a tiny cross as a grave marker. Another boy gave the "sermon," while the entire group sang.

The next day, remembering the fun of yesterday, they dug up the bird and repeated the ceremony. This was repeated for several mornings. But there came a time when the bad odor of the decaying bird stopped the funeral games.

Child's play? Maybe. But what about adults who constantly dig up the past, punishing themselves with yesterday's mistakes, hurting themselves with yesterday's memories?

In her book *Times to Remember,* Rose Kennedy wrote, "I prefer to remember the good times." She points out that she has known the joys and sorrows of a full life and that she can never reconcile herself to the tragedies. But she can look back selectively, using her energies to recall the good times.[2]

As a boy, I enjoyed playing with a magnet, picking up nails, pins, and other metal objects. The mind is like a magnet. We can sift through the past and drag up all the hurts and disappointments. Or we can remember the good times, especially on those black nights and gray mornings when our halos begin to fade.

5. *Believe in the brightness of tomorrow's halo.*

No one lives on a flat plane. Life is always up and down.

Joshua Liebman noted, "Every man is a little country with hills and valleys, summits and depressions."

When we're on the low side, we may deserve a medal just for getting out of bed. That's the time to remind ourselves that the darkest hour has only sixty minutes. Also, that just as the tides turn every twelve hours and twenty-five minutes, so a high tide is bound to follow a low one in our lives.

Charles L. Allen, renowned author, tells about a conversation with a fellow minister, who was eighty-seven. He has read a chapter in the Bible every day since he learned to read. Since he had lived daily with the Bible for over eighty years, Allen was anxious to know his friend's favorite verse. "You'll find my favorite passage fifteen or twenty times, scattered here and there," he said. Then he quoted Exodus 12:41, "And it came to pass. . . . " The elderly minister continued, "I have lived long enough to know that verse is true, that all things do come to pass." He explained that the heartaches, the disappointments, and even the joys all come to pass. Nothing comes to stay.

Enrico Caruso, incomparable Italian tenor, had one of the most brilliant voices in the history of music. He mastered at least sixty-seven operatic roles, and his repertoire included about five hundred numbers. Recordings of his matchless voice are still enjoyed by music lovers everywhere.

Early in his career, Caruso was standing in the wings, fearfully waiting for the curtain to rise. The stagehands were surprised to hear him mutter to himself, "Get out of my way, you little me. I'm a big me, and I need room to get out on that stage." This was Caruso's way of mustering courage, his way of polishing his halo in a moment of fear.

So long as our motive is right, there's nothing wrong with reminding ourselves that tomorrow's curtain may rise on a bigger me.

   6. *Act as if your halo were healthy.*

Even if you feel worthless, act as if you were at least marketable, if not priceless!

Alfred Adler (1870-1937), an Austrian psychiatrist, said, "By changing our opinions of ourselves, we can also change ourselves." This means that to feel right, we must act right. Feelings follow actions. Act afraid, and we'll be afraid. Act daringly, and we will feel daring. This means that how we react to what happens is more important than what happens. The key issue is not whether my ego is hurting, but whether I act as if it were hurting.

In December of 1955, a black seamstress in Montgomery, Alabama, acted as if she were a person of worth, even though custom and society told her she was a second-class citizen.

Forty-two-year-old Rosa Parks was riding a bus home from work. She performed an impulsive act of civil disobedience by refusing to yield her front-of-the-bus seat to a white man. The incident led not only to her arrest (she was fined ten dollars) but also to the birth of a landmark civil-rights campaign led by Martin Luther King, then an obscure young preacher in Montgomery.

"To me it was not a big thing to keep my seat," Rosa Parks recalled years later. "I wasn't afraid. I was a little annoyed and resigned more than anything else. And worried because I couldn't get home to my husband and mother."

Standing up for something often takes courage. In this case, remaining seated took courage. But the fact is, Rosa Parks *did* something.

If you're browbeaten, your halo's fading, and you fear you've reached zero on the scale of self-esteem, don't wallow in the martyr's mire. Do something! And in the doing, your self-image will regain its rightful status.

On the other hand, if you're determined to worry over your halo, go off by yourself for a brief time and worry. But don't ruin a whole week. Select a day, or better yet just an afternoon, and get your worrying over with for a week.

Attitude is the mind's paintbrush. It can color a situation gloomy and gray or cheerful and gay. Attitudes are more important than facts, especially when you're dealing with halos.

Notes

1. C. S. Lewis, *Mere Christianity* (New York: Macmillan, 1969).

2. Rose Kennedy, *Times to Remember* (Garden City, New York: Doubleday, 1974).

5
When You're Tired of Being Phony

Methuselah, the oldest man in the Bible, lived to be 969. About all we know of him is that his father, Enoch, "walked with God: and he was not; for God took him" (Gen. 5:24), and that Noah was Methuselah's grandson. His life had length but whether it had depth or breadth is a mystery.

The desire to live for many, many years is natural. But few are satisfied just to live a long time. We desire depth and maturity. We seek freedom from phoniness and shallowness.

As children, we were satisfied to sail our toy boats in shallow bathtubs. But as mature adults, we long to float an oceangoing vessel. We hunger to be real persons.

What is a real person? I wish I had a simple answer. One of the best definitions comes from Eugene Kennedy, who teaches at Loyola University in Chicago. In his book, *A Time for Being Human,* Kennedy wrote that God doesn't work great signs in the skies for most of us. Whatever God accomplishes through human beings, he does so through ordinary ones, for most of us are ordinary.

What can ordinary persons offer? According to Kennedy, one of their best gifts to the world "is the simple sense of how to live deeply and lovingly." Life is more a question of who we are, not what we do.[1]

Genuineness has to do with being, more than doing. True, many genuine people are achievers. But all kinds of people "achieve" who are shallow and artificial.

Since we're dealing with concepts which are difficult to explain or understand, this chapter is made up of three true stories. I selected these three because they reveal persons who, in my opinion, were genuine. From their examples, maybe we can find escape from our own phoniness.

The first story is about the late William H. Danforth, who crossed my life for about five minutes when I was a teenager. I met Mr. Danforth one summer when I spent two weeks at Camp Minewanca on the eastern shores of Lake Michigan. It was a fun-filled, Roman-candle kind of summer that lit up a brief period of my adolescence.

I lived in Marion, a small town of 10,000 in southern Illinois, and this was one of my first long trips. I boarded the Illinois Central in nearby Carbondale on a Sunday afternoon. Late that night I changed trains in Chicago for Muskegon, Michigan. During the three-hundred-mile ride up the center of the state, I saw the sprawling campus of the University of Illinois at Champaign, the endless rows of corn and soybeans in the black Midwestern soil, and finally the tall, imposing skyline of the Windy City. All of this was in marked contrast to the quiet, tree-lined streets of home where we could walk nearly anywhere. At the crowded Union Station in Chicago, it looked to me as if everyone in town had suddenly decided to leave.

I had delighted in my provincialism. Mom and Dad never lived more than 12 miles from where they were born. My grandmother Sarah Gordon never saw the streets of Saint Louis, just 120 miles away.

I loved our little town in "Bloody Williamson" County. The town square was surrounded by F. W. Woolworth, the Orpheum Theater, Bainbridge Jewelry, Powell's Best Clothes in Egypt, Cline-Vick Drug Store, and the Greyhound Bus Station. From anywhere in town, you could hear the courthouse clock toll the hour and the half hour, day or night. Our simple life in the thirties revolved around the opening and closing of school, the county fair, family dinners, high school basketball games, Baptist revivals, medicine shows, Memorial Day parades, and Saturday afternoon matinees.

I rode where I pleased on my bicycle, content if I had ten or fifteen cents spending money a week for an occasional Coke and ice cream bar at Winnie Winkle's Cafe (operated by one of my cousins, whose name *was* Winnie—but not Winkle; her last name was Hamlet).

Our nation was just emerging from the Great Depression. Although the depression was nationwide, the Federal Government identified the three-county area where I lived as one of the fifty most-depressed areas in the nation.

Recently I scanned some 1938 issues of the *Marion Daily Republican*. The ads tell the story. One grocery ad offered sliced bacon for 25¢ a pound, head lettuce for 9¢, a pound of ground beef for 15¢, and two cans of chili for 25¢.

At J. B. Heyde and Sons you could buy a new, push-button Philco radio for $59.95. Or down the street at the Swan Motor Company, a new 1939 Plymouth for $742, which you could drive around the corner and fill up with gas at 19¢ a gallon.

The Illinois Brokerage offered curtain remnants at 1¢ each, and Pepperell bed sheets for 79¢. The Atwood Mine on the Spillertown hardroad delivered a ton of coal for $2, and Speed's News Stand sold a Greyhound ticket to Saint Louis for only $1.55.

That summer at camp, I was just breaking out of my world and discovering that not everyone lived like we did in a depressed, coal-mining community.

This camp attracted many boys from more affluent backgrounds than mine. I was there only because the American Youth Foundation gave me a scholarship. I was impressed with the abundance of wholesome food, especially the endless supply of cold milk served from gleaming, aluminum pitchers. Most of the boys were better dressed and more worldly-wise than I was.

Camp Minewanca was the prettiest place I had seen. Overlooking Lake Michigan, thirty-five miles north of Muskegon, its four hundred acres sprawled over wooded sand dunes. The giant pine trees had been dropping their needles for generations, and I can still imagine the crunch of the needles under my feet on the scenic Potawatomi Trail. William H. Danforth, a cofounder of the American Youth Foundation, lent the money to buy the original acreage.

We campers were organized into Indian tribes. Our activities emphasized sports and competitiveness. I remember the huge stone council circle where leaders challenged us to be our best, both mentally and morally. I remember the games and parties, stressing social needs, and worship in the stunningly designed log church.

We did a lot of group singing in the council ring, while the pine trees rustled overhead and the sunlight warmed our backs. This is one of the songs I remember:

> On the sand dunes of Minewanca,
> We'll sit in the sun
>   and get blisters on, on, on . . .
>
> Oh, hambone is sweet!
> Chicken am good!
> Possum meat is very, very fine.
> But give me, oh give me,
> I really wish you would,
> That watermelon hanging on the vine.

Although such camps are common today, this was an uncommon experience for me. It was a new and beautiful world, and I was challenged for the first time to be well-rounded, to be a real person. Growing up, I'd been taught at school to grow mentally. At church, the challenge was spiritual. But here it was offered as a package.

Roused at dawn from warm beds, we pulled on swimming trunks, still wet and cold from yesterday, and ran down the steep dunes to the beach. After warm-up calisthenics, our athletic director cried, "All right, boys, do you see those icebergs out there? Now all of you, into the lake and back to your tents to get dressed for breakfast." As much as we dreaded it, every boy had to jump in and completely submerse himself at least once. But climbing back up the dunes, with teeth chattering and shivering with goose bumps, I had the glorious feeling I could do anything!

The first morning, we were lined up in front of the administration building. A kindly gentleman in his seventies walked up to me and stuck out his hand.

"Hello," he said in a merry tone, "I'm William Danforth from Saint Louis." That was my first time to see a real millionaire. Oh, I'd heard there were millionaires, but I'd never seen one. The chairman of the board of the Ralston Purina Company was talking to me!

I was so overwhelmed all I could say was, "I'm Bob Hastings from Marion, Illinois." Danforth then gave me a copy of his famous little book with the red cover, *I Dare You*. I didn't even think to ask for his autograph.

Later, Danforth posed for a snapshot with me and the other fellows in Tent #47. I often look at that little photo pasted in the front of the book he gave me. Mr. Danforth is wearing a friendly smile topped by a distinguished-looking mustache. His hair is white and thin. He is short and slight, shorter than some of the teenagers standing beside him.

Og Mandino, author of *The Greatest Salesman in the World*, listed the twelve greatest books on motivation.[2] *I Dare You* is on that list. Danforth published the book privately to give to young people all over the world. Its thesis is simple: I dare you to build a well-balanced life. Its motto is: Think tall, smile tall, live tall, and stand tall. To appreciate Danforth's four ideals, you must know his roots.

Born in 1870, Will Danforth grew up in Charleston, Missouri. When he was fourteen, his parents sent him to Saint Louis to the Manual Training School, evidently because no local high school was available.

Like most youngsters from the undrained, swampy parts of Missouri, Will suffered frequent attacks of malaria. One day at school, a favorite teacher, George W. Krall, asked Will what he was doing about his chills and fever. Will said he took some medicine, but it didn't help much. Then Krall challenged him:

> I dare you to be the healthiest boy in the class. I dare you to chase those chills and fevers out of your system. I dare you to fill your body with fresh air, pure water, wholesome food, and daily exercise until your cheeks are rosy, your chest full, and your limbs sturdy.[3]

Will took the dare and adopted a set of lifelong rules dealing with high-protein food and exercise. He completed Washington University in Saint Louis, then founded and built the Ralston Purina Company into one of the leading corporations of the nation. By 1979, annual sales had climbed to over four billion dollars.

Danforth revolutionized the feeding of livestock and poultry, helping make America the best-fed nation in the world, under the banner of the red-and-white Purina checkerboard.

Long before the coffee break was invented, Danforth led daily calisthenics for his employees. He expected people to be healthy and outgoing. He never asked, "How do you feel today?" lest someone start thinking about his aches and pains.

Danforth was also an active churchman, serving as Sunday

School superintendent of the Pilgrim Congregational Church in Saint Louis. He achieved wide publicity in reaching boys and girls. In one contest, he gave away live, baby alligators which he shipped from a vacation trip in Florida!

For sixty years, Danforth's home at 17 Kingsbury Place in Saint Louis was a center of hospitality for prominent ministers, authors, businessmen, lecturers, actors, missionaries, and hunting friends. A grandson, John C. Danforth, later became Attorney-General for Missouri, and then a US senator from Missouri.

As a boy in Sunday School, I had memorized Luke 2:52, "And Jesus increased in wisdom and stature, and in favour with God and man." But until I saw those virtues spelled out in *I Dare You,* I did not see the value of a balanced life.

Oh, I don't mean William Danforth "revolutionized" my life. He didn't inspire me to found a great corporation. He did encourage me to be Bob Hastings, to be myself, to be genuine, if not "successful."

Through the years, Danforth's personality has been an un-conscious influence on me. Whenever I drive by Checkerboard Square in Saint Louis, I remember Danforth's challenge, "I dare you to be Bob Hastings; dare you to be real."

My second illustration, unlike Danforth, is drawn from poverty and slavery. I'm indebted to the late Ruby Berkley Goodwin for it.

Ruby grew up in Du Quoin, another Illinois mining town about thirty-five miles northwest of Marion. Her book, *It's Good to Be Black,* describes small-town life in Du Quoin in the years preceding World War I.[4]

Among other stories, Ruby includes one about her great-grandmother Judy, a slave on an Alabama plantation. Judy's master, John Hopgood, wanted to breed her with a healthy, young buck of his choice. Judy refused to be coerced and ran off and hid in the swamps. For three years, she saw only the few brave slaves who slipped into the woods after dark to bring her bits of food and beg her to come home.

" 'Taint safe, Judy. 'Taint safe for a lone 'oman," they warned.

But Judy claimed she wasn't scared. "In-a da daytime Ah make frens wid da animals. Ain't nothin' wild effen you kin ta'k hits own ta'k."

Then she described the nights:

"De night ain't bad nuther, caise Ah allers knowed how to ta'k wid Jesus. But in de Swamps, Ah done learnt to let Jesus ta'k to me."

Did Judy's life have a happy ending? It depends on your definition of happiness. Here's how it turned out.

After a few months, Mr. Hopgood called his slaves together to announce: "If any of you-all know where that olde sow Judy is hidin', you can tell her to come on in. Ah don't aim to beat her no mo' but Ah'm sellin' her on down the river. Now get on back to the field."

Ruby Goodwin says a new song was born that day on the plantation. The ugly mask of fear was ripped away while the slaves sang:

> Hit's a hard road, chillun,
> Hit's a hard road, chillun,
> Hit's a hard road, chillun,
> Hit's a hard road, chillun,
> But dere's joy, joy, comin' bye an' bye.
>
> De Hebrew chillun went through fiah,
> Crossed ovah Jordan an' didn't nevah tiah,
> Caise dey knew Jehovah was in de sky
> An' dere's joy, joy, comin' bye an' bye.

The next morning, Judy walked into the backyard of the big

house. Two days later they chained her to an ox cart and marched her off to a nearby auction. But great-granddaughter Ruby says Judy's head was high! A shallow person would have stumbled.

A third example of genuineness comes from *Donahue: My Own Story,* by Phil Donahue, the highly admired TV talk host. Donahue describes an assignment early in his career, when he was trying to make a name for himself. He was to cover a mining accident in Holden, West Virginia, where thirty-six miners were trapped underground.

As rescue teams emerged, soot covering their faces, worried relatives gathered. It was 2:30 AM and snow covered the ground. A local preacher said, "Dear God, let us pray." Then the people joined hands and began singing,

> What a friend we have in Jesus;
> All our sins and griefs to bear;
> What a privilege to carry
> Everything to God in prayer.

Donahue said the beautiful scene gave him goose bumps. He could just see the scene on the evening news. However, the cold had thickened the oil in his camera, dragging the film. By the time he held the camera close to his body so as to warm and thin the oil, the song and prayer were over.

Knowing his was the only network there, Donahue begged, "Reverend, I'm from CBS news; could you please go back through your prayer? We have 206 TV stations across the country who will hear you and millions will pray for your miners."

The mountain preacher replied, "Son, I just couldn't do it. I've already prayed to my God, and any other praying at this time would be wrong. No sir, I just can't do it."

Donahue persisted, "But Reverend, I'M FROM CBS NEWS!" But to no avail.

In shock over the disappointment, Donahue walked to a pay phone, dialed CBS in New York and blurted out, "The __ __preacher won't pray."

Driving to work one morning a year or two later, Donahue realized that the preacher's stand was the greatest demonstration of moral courage he'd ever seen. Here was one minister who wouldn't put on a show for Jesus or sell his soul for CBS TV. "I don't know where he is now," Donahue concluded, "but if he isn't going to heaven, no one is."[5] The preacher's example, on that cold morning on the mountain, was a pronouncement of genuineness.

When you fear phoniness in your life, one of these three may help you: William Danforth, who dared to stand tall; Judy, who dared to stand for conviction; or the mountain preacher, who dared to stand for integrity.

Notes

1. Eugene Kennedy.

2. Og Mandino, *The Greatest Salesman in the World* (New York: Fell, 1967).

3. George W. Krall as quoted in William Danforth, *I Dare You* (Saint Louis, 1942), p. 1.

4. Ruby B. Goodwin, *It's Good to Be Black* (Carbondale, Illinois: Southern Illinois University Press, 1976), pp. 52-53.

5. Phil Donahue, *Donahue: My Own Story* (New York: Simon & Schuster, Inc., 1980), pp. 65 *ff*. Used by permission.

6
When a Wedding Isn't Enough

Our son married while I was writing this book. To my surprise and pleasure, he asked me to speak a personal word at the wedding. As a minister, I had performed many marriages, with the traditional "Do you take this man. . . . this woman?" liturgy. But to lay aside the rituals and just talk informally to the couple before me at the altar was a new experience.

I condensed my deepest feelings about the home into a short statement. I tried to be practical, knowing that although some marriages may be made in heaven, all of them must be lived out on earth. Also, I spoke with the awareness that the altar and the attorney's office are now almost even in the volume of business they do, with fewer and fewer steps between courtship and the courtroom.

I began with David and Vera Mace's definition of *wedding* "A wedding is not a marriage. A wedding is only the beginning of an undertaking that may or may not, someday, develop into a marriage."

I quoted the Mace's analogy of a garden, pointing out that on their wedding day, no couple has a magic key to a beautiful garden. At best, they are given an empty lot, a few seeds and garden tools, and the rest is up to them.

It is much easier to be pronounced husband and wife than to *become* husband and wife. The pronouncement takes only minutes; the becoming takes years. Contrary to what some think, marriage is a school we enroll in, not a course we complete as soon as we say, "I do."

A wedding is like Christmas, replete with ribbons and bows, candles and starlight, family and warmth, excitement and togetherness. But a marriage includes the workdays, as well as the holidays, and some nights with no stars and some dinners with no candlelight. If a marriage is to be lasting and meaningful, it must be forged in the crucible of everyday living, not in the tinsel of Christmas.

The reason I shared these thoughts with my son and new daughter-in-law was that our thinking about love seems to be fuzzy. We have trouble sorting out the difference between the romanticism of the wedding day and the realism of the next day and the next day and the next day and the next day.

In his book, *Half Way Up the Mountain*, psychiatrist David C. Morley warns, "One of the real problems of the process of marriage is that it begins at too lofty a plane. It begins at what, in too many instances, is the zenith of the relationship. All movements from then on are down. . . . All of us were raised on stories about the beautiful princess and the handsome prince who, after many fiery trials, were finally married and lived happily ever after."[1]

Morley goes on to explain that if one starts any journey from the ultimate peak, there is only one way to go—down. Certainly a couple should see their wedding day as a "mountain peak experience," but only in the sense that other peaks, even loftier and more promising, loom in the distance.

Years ago I copied a quotation by F. Alexander (I failed to note his first name or where I read the quotation). Anyway, it captures the secret of how to move from a wedding to a marriage:

> Love is a passionate and abiding desire on the part of two . . . people to produce together the conditions under

which each can be and spontaneously express his real self;
to produce together an intellectual soil and an emotional
climate in which each can flourish, far superior to what
either could achieve alone.

Enough for the ideal. Instead, let's talk about how any couple
can help themselves climb from the initial peak of their wedding,
on up the slopes to vistas yet undreamed.

These suggestions come from my own thirty-five year marriage. Books and professional counselor can offer other advice.
My ideas are mere starters.

1. *A home is not a reformatory.* If your wedding vows ever
materialize into a satisfying marriage, you must once and for all
renounce the temptation to make your mate over in your image.
This is one of the most profound insights into marriage, but is
commonly overlooked because of its simplicity.

True, the Bible says, "God created man in his own image"
(Gen. 1:27). But you and I are not God.

Some of us have a neurotic need to be "fixers," playing God
with other people's lives, smothering them in our preconceived
ideas of what's "best" for them. This is seen in all walks of life, not
just marriage. But it is doubly deadly between husbands and
wives. During courtship, we major on our similarities and delight
in learning how much alike we are. But once we marry, the differences become more apparent. This is good, of course, for who
would want to be married to someone exactly like himself or herself?

Some men, who idolized their mothers, try to make another
"Mom" out of their wives. Some women, who idolized their
fathers, try to make another "Daddy" out of their husbands. But
again, who wants to be married to his own mother? Who wants to
be married to her own father? The whole idea is sick. Until a couple unmasks such effort to remake the other as a sickness, they

are in for a lot of trouble spelled with a capital *T*.

Certainly people should grow and mature in marriage. Each mate should seek to correct irritants in his or her life. Neither partner will consciously follow patterns that are contrary to the morals, taste, or ideals of his or her mate. But the change will occur as each mate sees his or her own faults and out of love and consideration takes steps to change. But it's a me-changing-me and not a me-changing-you pattern.

Change, unless entered into voluntarily, can only end in resentment. One of the saddest sights is a mousey husband completely made over by his wife or a clinging wife wholly dominated by her husband. A warm and satisfying marriage springs from the union of two persons, not one person and one robot.

And no one can be a person without personhood, which is another word for uniqueness. What if all "musical notes" sounded the same? What if every color in the "rainbow" were identical? What if we could only make one vocal sound? There'd be no music, no "rainbow," no language. Only monotony! That's exactly what you have in a marriage when either partner embarks on a crusade to reform the other.

As a writer, I spend a lot of time at the typewriter, but I detest carbon paper. I don't like the smudges! The problem with trying to make your mate a carbon copy of yourself is that it smudges your entire relationship.

In his book, *Straight Talk to Men*, James C. Dobson describes an early frustration in the life of Joyce Landorf. What really made Joyce furious was her husband's inevitable question, "Joyce, did you lock the back door?" She always said yes, whereupon Dick still walked to the door to verify that it was locked. Did Dick think Joyce was lying? Or did he think she didn't have the brains to remember she'd locked the door.

Dobson says Joyce then felt an impression from the Lord. "Take a good look at him, Joyce. I have made your husband a door-checker. He's a detail man. That's why he's such a good banker. He can instantly spot errors which others overlook. Yes, I made Dick a 'door-checker,' and I want you to accept him that way."[2]

When I read that story, I immediately saw myself, for I'm an inveterate door-checker, thermostat-setter, checkbook balancer, and clock-watcher. I'm sure this is often an irritant to my wife, Bessie, especially when we're leaving for a trip and, after a few blocks, I turn and drive back to see if our automatic closer really shut the garage door! But fortunately for both of us, she's let me be that way. And surprisingly, I've made some changes on my own.

Bessie sometimes says to me, "Bob, I wish I could cook like your mother."

I reply, "But I didn't marry you to cook like Mom. I married you for yourself. Sure, she was a good cook. But I enjoy the flair with which you light a candle when we sit down to eat, even on ordinary occasions. My mother never did that."

Loving mothers put warm food on the table, but loving wives know how to light warm candles as well. If I had to choose (and I don't), I'd rather have a little candlelight in my marriage along with scorched toast, than all the hot biscuits in the world.

Moms are good and wives are good. Dads are good and husbands are good. But neither is good when the roles are switched.

2. *Taking each other for granted is wrong.* To accept one's mate as he or she is does not mean aloofness. It is not a live-and-let-live, couldn't-care-less attitude. Just because we feign blindness when looking at the faults of our mates does not mean we must also be blind to their strengths. The biggest "sin" in marriage is slipping into the rut of taking each other for granted.

One of the simplest ways to help your marriage is to seize opportunities to praise and compliment your mate. No gift, however expensive, is a substitute for a spoken word of appreciation.

Studies show this is true on the job: Employees need spoken approval, as well as dollars from their employers.

A distraught husband told his pastor, "Reverend, when you preach her funeral tomorrow, I want you to say she was the finest woman a man ever had."

The minister replied, "I will, John, because it's true; but why didn't you tell her while she was living?"

We use shoe polish and furniture polish, but the best polish is what we use to shine each other's halos. Elbow grease spent on polishing the self-image of a mate is always retroactive, for the new brightness has a way of warming and lighting your own life.

If your spouse grew up with a poor self-image, then the need for reassurance is probably double. To tell an individual who already feels beaten that he is no good only reinforces such negative feelings. If anyone lacks confidence to begin with, and then a mate grabs every chance to belittle her, what little ego which remains is soon swept away.

Mary Lamb, the sister of essayist Charles Lamb, became mentally incompetent. In this state, she often asked, "Why is it that I never seemed to be able to do anything to please my mother?"

And John Newton made the poignant statement, "I know my father loved me—but he did not seem to wish me to see it."

Fortunate is the family where the parents constantly reinforce each other, as well as their children, by saying, "I believe in you; I'm for you; I'm pulling for you; I'm your best friend."

I've often said in my preaching that one of the best ways to multiply yourself is to find someone who's doing a good job and encourage him. Someone who knows he is appreciated will try to do more!

Cold water is good for a lot of things, such as quenching thirst on a hot day. But don't go around throwing cold water on the egos of those you claim to love. People get enough hard knocks in life without being put down within the walls of their own homes. If an important guest came to your home, would you peck away at his weaknesses and imperfections? Would you insult him? Of course not. You'd show an interest in his work and make complimentary statements. You'd help him feel some of the importance he deserved. Now look at it this way. Isn't your spouse the most important person in your life? If so, he or she deserves even greater courtesy and respect.

Here's a little mental exercise. The next time you're away from your spouse, even for a few hours, remind yourself, "I'm just about to meet the most important person in my life." Note I didn't say the most important person in the world, for that might not be true. But it is true that if marriage is worth anything, it's worth choosing a mate who means more to you than anyone else. Otherwise, it's a cheap contract.

3. *Staying is harder than getting there.* I'm indebted to L. D. Johnson, chaplain of Furman University in Greenville, South Carolina, for the following insight from his book, *Moments of Reflection.*

Although Johnson is not discussing marriage, the principle applies. As an example, he used weight loss, quoting a friend who admitted, "In my time I must have lost several hundred pounds." Johnson also cited a study by a doctor which showed that 50 percent of patients who had lost weight gained it all back in two or three years. Moreover, 90 percent gained it all back after nine years.

"In almost anything we undertake, staying is harder than getting there," Johnson continued. "Most of us can generate enough enthusiasm and energy to make a good start, or a good impression, or begin a good relationship. It's keeping going that is hard. We run out of steam. When the novelty wears off we have to have a new challenge—a new job, a new town, a new partner."[3]

This illustration can be applied anywhere. It's easier for an athlete to get in shape than to stay there (ever notice the sloppy, middle-aged men who were fit and trim when they played in high school or college sports?) It's easier to join a church than to pursue a level of Christian maturity.

Getting a job is easier than holding on to a job. It's easier to plan a vacation trip than it is to enjoy it and come home refreshed. It's easier to make a friend than to hold one through thick and thin. It's easier to learn to drive than it is to chalk up a good driving record, year after year.

It's often easier to go to bed than to go to sleep, or to make a New Year's resolution than to keep it. It's easier to conceive a baby than it is to rear a youngster to maturity. It's easier to buy a garden spade than it is to raise cucumbers.

The analogy applies to marriage, right down the line. It's easier to say "I do" than to say "I will" to the constant, daily responsibilities of parenthood, wifehood, and husbandhood. "Let's go!" always excites us more than "Let's stay." Holding on demands more than grabbing hold.

As a boy I often heard friends and relatives comment on someone who was sick as "holding on." At the time, I never thought much of such a diagnosis. But I've changed my mind, for there are times when someone deserves a medal for just "holding on" in life.

One nice thing about "holding on" during the dark days is that life tends to go in cycles. If today's bad, it may be time for the pendulum to swing the other way. Many marriages that floundered might now be sailing in fairer seas had there been more patience on both sides, more determination to hold on, even when it seemed there was no chance of going on.

4. *Whole marriages don't spring from half-persons.* Ephesians 5:3 is a beautiful picture of marriage, "For this cause shall a man leave his father and mother, and shall be joined unto his wife, and they two shall be one flesh." Just as a believer finds one-

ness in Christ, so a committed couple finds oneness in each other.

But I'd like to point out an error that's crept into out thinking. Because two halves make one in mathematics, we've transferred this idea to husbands and wives. We assume that a man is only a half-person until he is married, and likewise a woman.

There is some truth in this. Happily married couples rightfully testify that they never knew completeness until they found it in each other. However, in our zeal to magnify the oneness of marriage, let's not overlook that it is a union of two whole persons, who continue as two whole persons. If a marriage were the union of two half-persons, neither could function in any respect without the other.

Marriage doesn't make Siamese twins out of a man and a woman. During sexual intercourse, they achieve unique oneness. In many other areas of their marriage, they sense a oneness of purpose and meaning. But each is still an individual, and each must be respected by the other as an individual.

I've never cared too much for the wedding ceremony in which the bride and groom each hold a candle and in turn light a third candle. Then they extinguish the first two candles as a symbol that they are now one.

There is much in this symbolism that is beautiful and touching. But if you carry this logic to its conclusion, it means each loses his identity and is now wholly merged with the other. I think this is shortchanging both parties.

The better symbolism would be for each to bring lighted candles together, so that the flames of the two merge into even a brighter and warmer light. But both candles continue to burn, each unique in its gifts and strengths.

If you subscribe to the theory of a one-candle marriage, you set the stage for one person dominating the other. If two people become one in every respect, both must be made identical. Thus, whichever is out of step must be "reformed."

In marriage, we need the strength of two persons, not two half-persons. A marriage should at least double our pleasure, our wisdom, our achievements. Also, children need a role model of a male who is a whole person, as well as a female who is a whole person. If children see their parents as a blur, as a blending of two into one, the male/female role model is destroyed.

Because, in a mystical and sexual sense, a couple becomes one, this does not mean that from hereon they look alike, feel alike, and think alike on every issue. In marriage, two whole and complete persons merge, but neither swallows up nor smothers the other.

5. *Intimacy is more than sex.* I've left this suggestion for last, as it's the hardest to define. I know what I mean, but feel uncertain in my ability to express it.

When we speak of being *intimate* with someone, everyone assumes we're talking about sex. And we often are, for sex is a key factor in intimacy. But sex is not the ultimate intimacy. Sex plays a key role on the stage of intimacy, but it never steals the show.

In our marriage, sex came much earlier than intimacy. I have no "studies" to back me up, but I'm certain this is true of everyone. The sex drive in normal persons is so strong that it surges ahead of our desire for intimacy. In fact, we may enjoy sex long before we're even aware of intimacy in its fullest sense. Some couples may *never* understand intimacy, much less experience it.

To me, intimacy means both closeness and distance. These may not be technical terms the marriage experts use, but they speak to me. At first, they seem contradictory. How can you be both close to and distant from someone? It's one of those mysteries of personal interaction, but I've found it to be true. The closer my wife and I have become, the more freedom we enjoy to be our own persons, to have breathing space. The greater the distance—that is, each being his own—the stronger the magnet of closeness.

First, let's talk about distance. Any gardener knows that one way to increase productivity is to increase the space between plants. An overzealous amateur, setting out his first tomato plants, might space them only two or three inches apart. But he soon learns that plants need space and distance, as well as moisture and nutrients. The domineering spouse who seeks to control every thought, every penny, every minute, or every action of the other is overlooking this vital principal in marriage. A home is not a prison, where every member is regimented by the stronger of two parents. Rather, a home is a spacious garden with room for all to mature and be themselves.

Whatever else love is, it's not using others as doormats. Walking roughshod over anyone, demanding my way, asserting my superiority, putting the other person down is anything but love.

Theologian John Hick says that God created man and set him at "epistemic distance" from himself. I think this phrase refers in part, to God giving man room and freedom to say either yes or no to his Creator.

Or as L. D. Johnson explains it in his book, *Moments of Reflection,* "Love cannot exist under compulsion. Faith is not faith unless unfaith is a genuine option. Relationship is rich and mutually fulfilling in direct proportion to its mutual voluntariness. Therefore, God . . . doesn't come on so strong as to overwhelm us."[4]

Distance in marriage does not mean aloofness or indifference. It does mean that neither mate "comes on so strong as to overwhelm the other." The ideal is "mutual voluntariness." In a good marriage, we're never bound with legal cords or dominant personalities. The cords—though they seem fragile to man—are woven of love and trust. If this sounds like pious language, so be it.

As an extreme illustration, imagine parents so proud of their firstborn that they determine to shield him from all that is harmful. So they construct a germfree, incubator-type, glass case for him. The temperature and humidity are carefully controlled, and the food measured exactly. As the child grows older, they hope to protect him for all bad influences, including the wrong kind of friends, racy magazines, offensive TV programs, and the like.

"He will be the world's first perfect youngster," they boast to their friends.

But what they call wisdom is actually foolishness, for there is no room for the youngster to grow. In a few years his limbs become twisted, and he looks more like a sideshow freak than anything.

I think you see the moral of my little story. There is no growth without choice, without alternatives. What's true of a baby in a cage is also true of a marriage in a straitjacket.

In my own marriage, I can think of two examples where we have edged closer to intimacy through distance. I travel a great deal in my work. In all of my ministry, I've lived on an uncertain schedule. When I come home, my wife could ply me with endless questions of where I've been, whom I've seen, what we said. If I were late, she could be walking the floor, peering out the windows, worring what in the world had happened to me. Had I been in a wreck? Was I lying somewhere unconscious beside the highway?

Instead, we have an understanding that I'll be home when I am home. I give an approximate arrival time, but I don't feel hurried and pressed if I'm late. If she gets sleepy, she goes to bed, assuming I have sense enough to find my way home. She has always encouraged me to stop at a motel if the weather turns bad or I'm delayed, rather than rushing to arrive home at some exact moment. Flexibility, not rigidity, is the pattern.

I can remember that when I was a teenager my mother would lie awake, listening for my steps or the slamming of the car door. But now I'm not a child, and I resent being treated like a child.

A second example from our marriage is money. When we were younger and the children were at home, we had one bank account. In recent years, with more money for discretionary spending, my wife established her own personal checking account. She uses this for her clothing, gifts, extra trips to visit our children, or whatever. It's not for our day-to-day household expenses.

I've never looked at her check stubs or opened her bank statements when they come in the mail. I feel strongly that each member of any family should have some "fun" money that's his to spend as he pleases, without accounting to anyone.

You might reply, "Well, if I didn't need to watch every nickel just to pay bills, I wouldn't review my wife's (or husband's) checkbook either." My answer to that is I've known men with no real money worries who still kept a tight rein on every dollar. Why? The real issue in such cases is not the amount of money but the desire to control. To some people, money is a symbol of power and, to some men, of masculinity. Controlling all of the money is an effort to control all of one's spouse.

I'm not saying wives should never worry when their husbands are late or that every family needs two or more checking accounts. I mention these only as examples of how my wife and I have learned to allow each other breathing space. This kind of distance enhances our closeness, for the same freedom to widen the space between us is also available to narrow such space. Closeness by choice (not coercion) is the only kind of closeness that makes for intimacy.

Closeness is more than physical nearness to the one you love. Physical nearness is part of a loving relationship, not its goal. In the fullest sense, before we can touch another's body, we must first touch his or her mind. If all I want is a sex partner, I can forget about intimacy. But if I want a meaningful marriage, in which sex is one of many factors, then I, as well as my mate, must know and be known.

How do we really get to know someone? Time is a basic ingredient. Early in my marriage, I probably would have said I knew my wife well. But compared to our intimacy today, after thirty-five years of marriage, we were more like strangers when we first spoke our vows. Intimacy takes time.

Long-term intimacy involves the sharing of minds, as well as bodies. The greater the self-revealing of the mind, the more intense and sexually fulfilling is the sharing of bodies.

It's much easier to reveal ourselves to someone we trust. Trust, too, requires time to mature. The more we trust someone, the more we share; and the more we share, the more we learn to trust. Both processes interact and reinforce each other.

Sharing has two faces: the telling side and the listening side. Some wives (and husbands) might tell more if their husbands (or wives) listened more. It's always easier to talk than to listen. You see this in everyday conversation. The next time you're in a group, notice how many people can't wait until they can grab the conversation, much like show-and-tell in kindergarten. People carrying on a group conversation often remind me of two or more cars at an intersection, each restless to jump the light and be the first to go.

While one person is talking, others are making mental notes of what they'll say as soon as the light turns green (or they can slip a word in edgewise)!

One must listen not only to what his partner is saying but also to what his partner is feeling. Too often we hear only the words because we're preoccupied with our own feelings.

At one point in our marriage, I felt I had to come up with a quick solution (Mr. Fixit!) to every problem my wife shared. It took me a long time to learn better. I came to realize that listening—just understanding how the other person feels, fears, or hurts—is also a part of the solution.

To be able to say, "I can understand how you feel," is sometimes more helpful than a quick solution. Not all problems have instant answers anyway.

The egotist has a difficult time ever finding closeness with a spouse. He spends all his energy talking or assuming he is the Mr. Superman of omniscience.

Even in sex, the egoist or narcissist is preoccupied with his satisfaction, for which his sexual partner is only a tool. Intercourse thus becomes less than *inter*course. Genuine intercourse demands the sharing of selves through our bodies.

Some couples never achieve intimate closeness because they don't try. One or both partners may fear intimacy, preferring the shell of aloofness. One spouse may fear that if the other really knew him, he would be rejected. Another spouse may be suspicious of intimacy because she never experienced it while growing up or never saw it in her own parents.

We know that we are approaching intimacy when we take the time and make the effort to know each other and then take steps to meet the needs which such intimacy reveals.

Richard Selzer, a surgeon, has written a book, *Mortal Lessons: Notes in the Art of Surgery*, of insights from his practice of medicine. One of the most touching scenes he describes is a young husband standing by the bedside of his wife. To remove a tumor in her cheek, Dr. Selzer also had to sever a tiny twig of the facial nerve. The surgery left her mouth twisted and clownish in appearance. Dr. Selzer tells how he watched the young couple.

"Will my mouth always be like this?" the young woman asked.

"Yes," Dr. Selzer replied, "it will. It is because the nerve was cut."

The woman was silent, but her lover-husband smiled. "I like it," he said. "It is kind of cute."

Selzer described what happened next: "Unmindful, he bends to kiss her crooked mouth, and I am so close I can see how he twists his own lips to accomodate to hers, to show her that their kiss still works. I remember that the gods appeared in ancient Greece as mortals, and I hold my breath and let the wonder in.[5]

If you can understand the four words, "the kiss still works," you know about all there is to know about intimacy. But if you don't know it, I have no other words to explain.

Tonight at the supper table, after I'd worked all day on this chapter, Bessie remarked that she has a "whole sack of candles" which she plans to melt down into one jumbo candle someday.

These candles are from our wedding, April 1, 1945. Through the years—all of our moves, the rearing of three children and seeing them off on careers and homes of their own— she held on to these candles. If I'd known it, I had forgotten it.

"We'll make them into one candle on one of our anniversaries—maybe our fortieth since our thirty-fifth has passed," she continued.

When the day comes when she strikes a match to that one candle, it will be the brightest and warmest candle of our lives. It's oneness will symbolize our long search for intimacy. Intimacy never comes on the wedding night. It comes only after years of understanding more and criticizing less, of giving more and demanding less, of trusting more and condemning less.

I began this chapter by describing my son's wedding. Now let me tell you about the prayer that ended the wedding.

After I knew Tim and Ginny were engaged, I ran across the following prayer from James C. Dobson's book, *Straight Talk to Men*. Dobson wrote that the prayer was written for his own wedding by his father, James Dobson, Sr.

I liked the prayer so much that I sent Tim a copy, which he chose for the benediction. I knew I was bound to choke up when I reached the opening lines. Printed programs allowed me to ask the congregation to offer the prayer in unison.

O eternal God: We bring Thee our children, Tim and Ginny. They were Thine but Thou in love didst lend them to us for a little season: to care for, to love and to cherish. It has been a labor of love and has seemed but a few days because of the affection we bear them. Fresh from thy hand they were, in the morning of their lives. Clean and upright, but yet two separate personalities. Tonight we give them back to Thee—no longer as two—but as one flesh. *May nothing short of death dissolve* the union here cemented. And to this end let the marvelous grace of God do its perfect work!

It is also our earnest prayer for them, not that God shall have a part in their lives, but that He shall have the pre-eminent part; not that they shall possess faith, but that faith shall fully possess them both; that in a materialistic world they shall not live for the earthly and temporal alone, but that they shall be enabled to lay hold on that which is spiritual and eternal.

Let their lives together be like the course of the sun: rising in strength, going forth in power, and shining more and more unto the perfect day. Let the end of their lives resemble the setting of the sun: going down in a sea of glory, only to shine on undimmed in the firmament of a better world than this.

In the name of the Father, and of the Son and of the Holy Ghost, Amen.[6]

Notes

1. David C. Morley, *Halfway Up the Mountain*

2. James C. Dobson, *Straight Talk to Men* (Waco: Word Books, Publisher, 1980), p.110.

3. L. D. Johnson, *Moments of Reflection* (Nashville: Broadman Press, 1980), p. 86.

4. Ibid., pp. 14-15.

5. Richard Selzer, *Mortal Lessons: Notes in the Art of Surgery* (New York: Simon & Schuster, Inc., 1976), pp. 45-46.

6. James C. Dobson, *Straight Talk to Men*, copyright © 1980, pp. 55-56; used by permission of Word Books, Publisher, Waco, Texas 76703.

7

When the Ice Melts Too Fast

On warm summer mornings in the thirties, before we owned an electric refrigerator, Mom hung an old-fashioned ice card in our front window. The card was black, with white lettering. In one corner was the number 100. In each of the other corners, 75, 50, and 25. A small hole in each corner made it easier to hang the card so the number you chose would be at the top.

The ice man drove down the street in his wagon or truck. When he spotted the ice card, he stopped. If the number fifty were at the top, the ice man chipped off a fifty-pound chunk of ice, slung it on his shoulder with tongs, walked around to the back door. He then walked into our kitchen, where he put it in our wooden ice box.

If Mom had just waxed her kitchen floor, she would lay down newspapers to catch the dripping water. The hotter the day, the more water dripped.

I've always remembered the trail of dripping water left by the ice man. That's why this proverb is so vivid to me, "Time—like ice—melts in transit."

Just as the ice man had less ice between his truck and our kitchen so we have less time when we pass certain milestones. Time can not be "saved," regardless of what anyone claims. (If someone boasts that he saved twenty minutes on a trip by taking a shortcut, ask him to give you part of those minutes!)

Horace Mann wrote, "Lost, yesterday, somewhere between sunrise and sunset; two golden hours, each set with 60 diamond minutes. No reward is offered, for they are gone forever."

Time is only used or misused. Unlike money, time cannot be saved and desposited, say, in a bank or safety deposit box. We may learn quicker ways to do things and thus have more time for other interests. Still, time is not "saved."

Benjamin Franklin said, "Dost thou love life? Then don't squander time, for that's the stuff life is made out of."

Time has fascinated me since I first learned the difference between the big hand and the little hand on our Big Ben alarm clock.

Henry W. Longfellow asked, "What is time? The shadow on the dial, the striking of the clock, the running of the sand, day and night, summer and winter, months, years, centuries—these are but arbitrary and outward signs, the measure of Time, not Time itself. Time is the Life of the soul."

Time is funny. Sit on a hot stove and a second will drag like a year! There was a time when every day had 24 hours, and that was that. But in the jet age, the day one flies East the day is shorter, while those flying West discover the day to be longer. On a Gemini flight, one astronaut saw 206 sunrises in 14 days. On a 6-day Apollo flight, he saw only 12. An astronaut returns to earth having aged a little less than the rest of us. The greater the velocity, the more aging is affected. According to some theories, if an astronaut stayed in space 20 of his years and came back, he would find all his family long since dead.

The technological age has greatly speeded up the way we live. A whole gamut of ways to do more in less time has been opened up. But still, no time is saved. Technology allows us to do more. Innovative people use these aids to increase their output. Technology has mastered the art of finding quicker ways to do things, but it has not found the art of spending time. One overriding problem in the year 2000 may be the question of purpose in a world of leisure.

Read these time-oriented words that are newcomers to our vocabulary: freeway, supersonic jet, computer, instant breakfast, laser beam, radio telescope, thermonuclear explosion, transistor, and videotape.

Faster and faster we go. Humankind has now achieved a top speed of 24,530 MPH through space (about 7 miles a second). Yet we have a long way to go, for at 36,000 MPH we would need over 11 years just to fly one way to Pluto. Some speeds are incomprehensible. A computer performs a function in five-billionth of a second. A TV screen flickers with 3 million dots per second. Meanwhile, the atomic clock at the US Bureau of Standards in Washington keeps dividing every earth-second into exactly 9,192,631,770 vibrations!

As a boy, I grew aware of the passing of time with the changing of the seasons. When I came home from school on February 14 and Dad was planting his lettuce bed, I knew spring was peeping over our shoulders. When I started going barefoot, I knew summer was near. When we put up our coal heater and gave it a coat of Black Camp Stove Polish, I knew winter was knocking at our door. And when Mom reached up to the top shelf of our pantry and took down a big cardboard box marked "Christmas decorations," I sensed the coming holidays.

In childhood, time creeps (remember how long it was from Thanksgiving to Christmas?). In our adult years, time marches. As we age, time flies. "My days are long," an elderly friend told me, "but a year's gone before I know it."

The great dividing line between success and failure can be expressed in five words, "I did not have time." This is a common excuse, and we use it every day, whether it's true or not. Many problems in life can be traced to mismanagement or misuse of time. This leaves us with a harried, frustrated feeling. What can you and I do about it?

First, I'm usually turned off by these so-called time-management experts with their graphs and charts. Oh, I know there's a place for time-and-motion studies, say in industry. But I said in the Prologue that I'm a nonexpert, giving ordinary advice to ordinary people. So to help you manage your time, I'll talk more about principles than techniques. Once you grasp the principles, you can work out the details in your own life.

1. *Time management is basically self-management.* This principle (like others I'll list) applies to money management as well. If we lack self-discipline, time and money will always be a problem.

Admittedly, much of our time is programmed for us by employers or by natural needs for eating, sleeping, and the like. It's in our discretionary time that we need the most self-control.

One of the rudest questions is for someone to ask, "Say, look at your calendar and see what you've got on for November 4." That person is about to make you feel guilty, by first getting you to admit you're free on that date, then asking you to give him that time.

This is about like a salesman first saying to you, "Say, look in your checkbook and see what your balance is." The question is not whether a day or an evening is free, but how should it be spent.

Unless I control my discretionary time, other persons or circumstances will step in and do it for me. We lose control of our time because we first lose control of ourselves.

2. *Decide on your values on life, then decide how you will budget your time to realize those values or goals.* Without long-term goals, you don't really need to manage your time because you're not going anywhere anyway. And, frankly, all kinds of people are in that boat. The last thing in the world they want is to calendarize their lives. All they do is shift into neutral and allow life to push them around. "Push them around" is correct, for these people go around in circles. They never cross the finish line.

James Russell Lowell compared life to a sheet of blank writing paper. And when I read him, I always sense the urgency of defining values:

> Life is a piece of paper white
> Whereon each one of us may write
> His word or two—and then comes night.
> Greatly begin! Though thou have time
> But for a line, be that sublime.
> Not failure, but low aim, is crime.

Stephen Vincent Benét spoke to the same theme:

> Life is not lost by dying! Life is lost
> Minute by minute, day by dragging day,
> In all the thousand, small, uncaring ways,

Although he stated it from a negative viewpoint, Mark Twain drew a vivid word picture of those who drift through life.

> A myriad of men are born; they labor and sweat and struggle for bread; they squabble and scold and fight; they scramble for little mean advantages over each other; age creeps upon them; infirmities follow; shames and humiliations bring down their prides and their vanities; those they love are taken from them, and the joy of life is turned to aching grief. The burden of pain, care, misery grows heavier year by year; at length, ambition is dead; pride is dead; vanity is dead; longing for release is in their place. It comes at last—the only unpoisoned gift earth ever had for them— and they vanish from a world where they were of no consequence, where they achieved nothing, where they were a mistake and a failure and a foolishness; where they left no sign that they have existed—a world which will lament them a day and forget them forever.

Before you look at the clock to budget your time, look deeply into a mirror to see what you really are and what you hope to be.

Then look through a telescope that peers far into tomorrow; catch a vision of where you want to go, the values that mold your life. Then—and only then—is there any need to think soberly about how to arrange the days and hours, the weeks and years, of your life.

3. *Recognize that nearly any project will take longer than you planned, just as nearly any expenditure will cost more than you think.* C. Northcote Parkinson, the witty British historian, spoke to this truth in two of his celebrated socioeconomic laws: Work expands to fill the time available. And expenditures rise to meet income.

I believe failure to understand this principle gets more people into trouble with the clock than any other factor. We simply don't allow ourselves enough time. We overprogram and overcommit ourselves. Family tensions erupt when members get too involved, too busy, too extended. We try to crowd twenty-eight hours into twenty-four, eight days into seven, and thirteen months into twelve. The result is emotional bankruptcy, frayed nerves, tension, and bickering.

The remedy? Allow more time than you think is needed. This is like planning to live on less than you earn. Any job takes a certain energy. But when we feel pressed and under tension, we use more energy than is needed. We end up more tired and irritable than necessary. Pity the individual who is always under pressure, always running late, always behind. He pays a double price.

Nearly every week my work carries me out of town, mostly by car. I've learned, to my profit, to budget a little extra time for each trip. If I figure a trip will take two hours, I allow about two-and-a-half hours. If it's a five-hour trip, I allow at least an extra hour. This gives me emotional breathing space.

If I encounter bad weather, heavy traffic, or other delays, I don't get as uptight. I try to leave in a relaxed frame of mind. This give me elasticity in my schedule and—best of all—in my mind.

I realize my job is unlike, say, a person who works an alloted number of hours per day and week. But some of the principles apply no matter what you have to do. Most of us would live longer and get more done if we learned to plan by the calendar, not the stop watch.

One other thing about my own schedule. When I take an engagement for a certain day, I look at my calendar to see if not only that day is clear but also if the day preceding and following are clear. I need time for planning and recuperating, as well as the doing. I do the same if it's a weekly engagement. What am I doing the week preceding? The week following?

For years, I have used a desk diary called, "Week at a Glance." In planning, I look at the week as a whole and never at a single day.

In summary, don't overextend. Don't overcommit. Don't play God. Don't say yes to every invitation. You may think you're indispensable, but you're probably the only one who feels that way! Here's a sobering thought: How many people would miss their next meal if they got the news of your sudden death?

4. *Cool efficiency isn't everything.* Don't be too hard on yourself if you suspect you waste too much time or bungle up your schedule. Some of the most disorganized folk are the most lovable and enjoyable to be around. So don't let the efficiency experts spoil your fun if, in your own way, you finally put together all the bits and pieces of life.

Life is a whole bundle of little things, not always neatly categorized. Life is neither a triumph nor a tragedy, but a long string of aggravations interspersed with gems of delight.

As human beings, we live in a world of missed connections, surprises, and breakdowns. We are not robots on a factory assembly line. It's OK to aim for efficiency, just don't become cold and mechanical.

I like what English novelist George Eliot said, in one of her works, about "the invasion of our private lives by the larger destinies of mankind." Our preciseness and punctuality must not harden us to the needs of others, who often cry out for us at inopportune times and inconvenient schedules.

In *A Time for Being Human*, Eugene Kennedy, one of my favorite authors, wrote: "We may never understand time if we are preoccupied with filling it in a puritanical and utilitarian fashion. Time that is lost is not necessarily time that is wasted."

Kennedy warned that if we watch our time the way an accountant watches his books, we may never be able to share ourselves or our time. "We may be oppressed with a sense that every bit of time must be accounted for down to the last second," he wrote. "God did not create the universe this way nor intend for his creatures to live in this manner."[1]

5. *Lists and unlists have their place.* We're back to the more practical suggestions. Making a daily list of jobs is one of the simplest, but most effective, ways to get through the day. So what if you don't complete the list by day's end? You'll still do more, with less lost motion.

For as long as I can remember, I've been a list maker. I mean by this that I get more done if I make a list. Sometimes I make a list for a week, but more often it's for a day. A list enables me to major on what's most urgent and to check off chores as they are finished. This way, I also minimize the risk of forgetting jobs I need to do. But I've about decided that keeping a list has disadvantages. A list makes it hard to say no to any demands anyone wishes to make of you. So recently, I decided to make an "unlist." That word (as a noun) is not found in the dictionary, but I decided that if the 7-Up people could coin a new word such as *uncola*, then I can invent the word *unlist*.

On my new "unlist" are the things I've decided to leave undone. Things that a few years from now won't matter a great deal anyway. When one reaches the end of life and makes a lifetime inventory, what he didn't do could be as meaningful as what he did. Life is too short to waste in petty trifles. As someone has said, "Don't make tragedies of trifles,/Don't shoot butterflies with rifles."

When we decide to leave out the nonessentials, we have more time and energy for what's really important. What makes it hard to make an "unlist" is our fear to say no to anyone. Since most of us crave the affection of other people, we're afraid to risk friendship by saying no, even if said in love.

But what it really boils down to is this: Saying no to trivialities makes it possible for us to say yes to potentialities.

6. *When you hit a crisis, keep a time-diary for a month.* Here is a practical piece of advice. If you're constantly meeting yourself coming back and lose all control over the clock and calendar, try keeping a time diary, say for a month. Write down exactly how you spend every segment of every day. Keep a record of the time spent biting your fingernails. Forget about efficiency; just keep tab of how you're floundering through life.

The value of the diary is looking at it once you've finished. You'll probably be amazed at the amount of time lost in indecision, the time thrown away in worry. Maybe, just maybe, such a diary will make you so disgusted with your work and play patterns that you'll do something about them. But I really can't say, for I've never kept such a diary myself.

7. *Allow time for cooling off.* Doing this will keep you out of a lot of trouble. If you're upset by someone and you feel like telling him or writing a nasty letter, sleep on it first. Avoid snap judgments of any kind. Impulsiveness is nearly always painful and sometimes fatal.

The other morning I was enjoying milk gravy made with bacon drippings. Now milk gravy is one of my weaknesses, whether it's made with the drippings of bacon, steak, chicken, hamburger, or sausage. That gravy looked so good and smelled so good that I took a big bite while it was still steaming hot. Yes, I burned my mouth and, for a day or two, suffered with little bits of skin peeling off.

This summer a teenager in our neighborhood poured gasoline into the tank of his lawnmower. Some of the gasoline spilled onto the hot engine and exploded, seriously burning the young man's face and arms.

Simple caution tells us to allow time for hot food or a hot lawn mower to cool off. It also tells us to let a hot temper cool down. Remember that anyone who can make you lose your temper has the upper hand.

8. *Live all your life.* As you program your life, don't box yourself in by saying that at age sixty-five or whatever, you'll forget about goals and values and just coast to the finish. Certainly, one can anticipate a more leisurely pace after retirement, but there's a difference between shifting gears and coasting.

Too many retirees die suddenly and for apparently little reason shortly after they retire. One cause may be the psychological shock of feeling that one is no longer needed. While this feeling is real with many, it is unjustifiable. It can be remedied. And one way is to keep on managing time, even though punching a time clock is no longer necessary.

According to the March, 1969, issue of "Sunny Side of the Street," more than 65 percent of the great achievements in this world are by persons who have passed their 60th birthday. The decade between 60 and 70 contains 35 percent of the world's greatest achievements. Between ages 70 and 80, it is 23 percent. And persons over 80 years of age claim credit for 8 percent of the world greatest achievements.

Michelangelo (1475-1564), one of the great artists and sculptors of all time, stayed productive until his death at the age of eighty-nine. Toward the end, he said, "I regret that I am dying just as I am beginning to learn the alphabet of my profession."

Pablo Picasso, ninety-one, was still painting within a few hours of his death in 1973. Twenty-six years beyond what we think of as normal retirement, Picasso was turning out paintings, etchings, sketches, lithographs, and sculptures. In his home alone, he left a greater wealth in modern paintings than are to be found in most of the world's museums.

Did Picasso continue to paint just because he was still around? Or did he have a relentless drive to stay productive that kept him alive to his nineties? Doctor Eric Pfeiffer, a psychiatrist at Duke University, says those who live longest are those who refuse to give in. They take old age in stride. They watch what they eat. They take long walks. They keep busy. "The decision to have an active life is really the important decision," Pfeiffer says. "It's a yes-saying to life."

Alexander Leaf, MD, studied three cultures where people live to advanced old age. He found these common factors in each: the aged are respected, they have simple eating habits, and employment is well beyond retirement age. Leaf interviewed one man, 108, who takes daily walks and complains that his children won't let him do more. Another 121-year-old man was helping his neighbor build a house.

Right now, America is youth-oriented. Youth is glorified in advertising, sports, the military, and even in government. The elderly are "expected" to sit and watch television. But statistics show that when a person sits down, he starts to die.

"Cast me not off in the time of old age" was the plea of Psalm 71:9. It is the plea of millions of people today. At least one step can be taken: Older people can stop feeling sorry for themselves and pick up a paint brush or at least go for a walk.

The late William Lyon Phelps has been quoted as saying:

> I know of no greater fallacy, nor one more widely be-
> lieved, than the statement that youth is the happiest time of

life. As we advance in years, we grow happier if we live in-
telligently. The universe is spectacular, and it is a free show.
Difficulties and responsibilities strengthen and enrich the
mind. To live abundantly is like climbing a mountain or a
tower. To say that youth is happier than maturity is like saying the view from the bottom of the tower is better than the
view from the top. As we ascend, the range of our views
widens. The horizon is pushed farther away. Finally, as we
reach the summit, it is as if we had the world at our feet.

If, after reading this chapter, you say I've said more about my
philosophy of life than time management, I guess you're right. But
to me, that's what time management is all about. I can't help but
feel some urgency about it, like Marshall Lyautey of France, who
was anxious to plant a certain tree.

His gardener replied, "There is no hurry—this tree is slow
growing and would not flower for a hundred years."

"In that case," replied the marshall, "plant it this afternoon."

Note

1. Eugene Kennedy, p. 15.

8
When the Dollars Won't Stretch

In 1975, John and Letha Scanzoni interviewed 3,096 husbands and wives and found that "33 percent reported money matters as the major area of marital disagreement." Child-related problems took second place, with 19 percent reporting their children as the major area of unhappiness.

Similar studies in the sixties showed the same. In a survey for *McCall's* magazine in 1964, George H. Gallup found money to be the chief source of quarreling between husbands and wives. And Dr. Joyce Brothers, writing in the November, 1964, issue of *Good Housekeeping* agreed that "American couples argue far more about money than any other issue."

When couples disagree over money, is that the real problem, or is it a cover-up for deeper, hidden conflicts? It is likely both. Like disagreements over in-laws, sex, discipline of children, religious differences, lack of common interest, and offensive personal habits, money can be the actual source of conflict. However, spatting over money is a socially accepted clothesline on which a troubled family can publicly hang its domestic troubles while the real problem lies elsewhere.

Singles face money worries too. The problem may simply be not enough dollars to go around or indecision over the use of the money, such as how much to save, where to invest, or what to spend it on.

In this chapter, I don't tell you how to set up a fool-proof budget or how to make a million dollars. I am not a financial expert. But I gladly share some basic principles that have helped me.

Money management starts with self-management. In the chapter on time management, I underscored the principle that self-discipline is essential. This is true whether one is managing the hours of the day or the dollars in a paycheck. If you lack self-discipline, you can never manage your bank account.

However, if a person cannot discipline his spending and saving pattern, someone will do it for him. Advertisers persuade him to buy this or that, and financial institutions provide him with credit. The undisciplined spender merely goes into the marketplace and buys until he reaches his credit limit, then submits himself to the payments as they come due. He's merely a bookkeeper of sorts, for his spending is predetermined each month by his creditors.

Spending patterns are based on values. Just as we invest time according to our values, so we spend money according to what we feel is worthwhile. The ultimate aim of money management is not to save, but to build our spending program around healthy goals. (Admittedly, if building up a large estate fits in with our values, then saving would be a top priority).

Money is neither moral nor immoral. Instead, like water, it is amoral, capable of either good or bad. Lost on a desert, with the temperature at 120°, water is not only good but also precious! But if one were drowning, water turns evil.

Money is a wonderful servant, but a poor master. As long as we remain in the driver's seat, telling the money where to go, we're secure. But when money gets the mastery over us, we're in for trouble. That's why I say values come before budgets.

The folly of wrong values is illustrated in the life of Hart P. Danks, a songwriter, who wrote "Silver Threads Among the Gold." The song was an unexpected hit, and the royalties poured in. Danks and his wife disagree over how to spend the newfound wealth. Separation followed. Danks died alone in a Philadelphia rooming house. Nearby was found an old copy of his song with these words written across it, "It's hard to grow old alone."

Danks's story is not extreme. In various patterns, it happens over and over when families or individuals misplace their values.

"The Materialist's Version of the Twenty-third Psalm" by Edward K. Ziegler echoes what I mean:

> Science is my Shepherd, I shall not want;
> He maketh me to lie down on foam-rubber mattresses;
> He leadeth me beside six-lane highways.
> He rejuvenateth my thyroid glands;
> He leadeth me in the paths of psychoanalysis for peace of
>   mind's sake.
> Yea, though I walk through the valley of the shadow of the
>   iron curtain, I will fear no communist; for thou art with
>   me; thy radar screen and thy hydrogen bomb, they
>   comfort me.
> Thou preparest a banquet before me in the presence of the
>   world's billion hungry people.
> Thou anointest my head with home permanents.
> My beer glass foameth over.
> Surely prosperity and pleasure shall follow me all the days of
>   my life; and I will live in Shangri-la forever.

Needs and wants sleep in different beds. No one goes far in money management until he can decide between the necessary and the desirable. This doesn't mean comfort is a sin or that self-denial is essential to budgeting. (One reason some people back off from money management is that they identify budgets with scrimping, rather than simply making the best use of what one has.)

A family—or individual— should first plan its spending to satisfy basic needs. Once these are met, go on to the wants. Problems occur when we reverse the two and spend too much on what we'd *like* to have, in contrast to what we *must* have.

Irene Prall of Dupo, Illinois, is one of the most resourceful persons I have met. Left with two little daughters and no pension or Social Security when her husband died of cancer in 1937, she determined to help herself. She worked as a newspaper distributor, seamstress, and bookkeeper to rear the little girls and see them through college.

I interviewed her in the fall of 1979, when she was seventy-three. She told me she was eating on thirty-five cents a day. I couldn't believe it until I went to her home, saw her big garden, her home-canned vegetables, and her deepfreeze running over. She buys only basics, such as sugar, flour, salt, coffee, and some meat.

"I have no wet garbage," she told me. "I eat every bite I cook. I plan my meals and get several meals, say, out of a chicken. I buy no prepared foods, ice creams, colas, or the like."

Her garden plot, which she enriched by hauling baskets of horse manure that someone gave her, bears in abundance, enough to share with neighbors.

Prall is the kind of person who can do anything. She was sixty-three when she bought her present home. It was a "wreck." She tore the walls down to the studs, rewired the house, and put in new plumbing. She put in a new subfloor and carpeting and dry wall throughout. Moreover, she partitioned the house into a duplex, for added income! She can lay blocks, paint, or nail on roofing.

Is she a miser? Is she poverty-stricken? Does she feel like a martyr? Hardly. She's been to Hawaii twice and to Europe. She was planning a trip to Israel!

She told a reporter for the *St. Louis Post-Dispatch* that she "has no use for talk about problems of the elderly struggling on fixed incomes." She added, "If I can, they can."

Admittedly, Irene Prall is exceptional. I don't use her to club those who are less innovative. But what she can do on a big scale, all of us can do on a small scale. She has learned to help herself in meeting basic needs and, in so doing, has found a surplus to satisfy her wants. "I don't want much," she told me. "This is the way I was reared."

Most things eventually cost more than you think. This is such a simple truth, yet so profound. Whatever it is—a vacation trip, roofing the house, or braces for Junior's teeth—inevitably cost more than we plan. This principle is kin to a similar one about time—most projects take more time than we allow.

Planning to spend exactly (or more) than we earn always ends up in frustration. If we spend less than we make, we have a cushion of money for the car battery that dies suddenly on a January morning or a tax audit that shows we underpaid.

Admittedly, this principle holds little comfort for the family on a bare-bones budget, where every penny is committed to basics.

In his book, *The Richest Man in Babylon,* George S. Clason quotes Arkad, who supposedly lived in old Babylon. Arkad was noted far and wide for his great wealth, liberality, and generosity with his own family. Each year his wealth grew to be more than he could spend. His friends persuaded him to share his secret. He said: "A part of all you earn is yours to keep." He had learned this from an older man, who became rich by "paying himself first."

His secret, of course, is another way of saying, "Live on less than you make." Arkad further said, "Enjoy life while you are here. Do not overstrain or try to save too much. If one-tenth is as much as you can comfortably keep, be content to keep this portion. Live otherwise according to your income and let not yourself get niggardly and afraid to spend. Life is good and life is rich with things worthwhile and things to enjoy."[1]

Budgeting is not the same as saving. Remember, we plan our spending to achieve our goals, not necessarily to have more money to save. The shrewd shopper who always sniffs out the cents-off bargains is not necessarily a wise money manager. More-over, what we do with what we buy is as important, or more so, than what we pay originally. If we waste food in the kitchen, it does little good to save at the supermarket. If we buy clothing just because it's on sale, we realize no real saving if the item is the wrong size, poor fit, shoddy workmanship, or soon out of style.

More money is not necessarily the answer. Ask the typical person how much money he needs and he'll likely say, "Just a lit-tle bit more." But wants have a way of out-distancing our income. The more we earn, the more we tend to want. This is why one's standard of living is not necessarily synonymous with his level of income. Some people make-do on much less and enjoy it far more, while others, with high incomes, mismanage and end up having less.

Each spending plan must be tailor-made. I prefer the words *spending plan* since *budget* has such negative overtones for many. (They say it's a bad word, for you can't "budge it"!) There is no such creature as an "average" budget or spending pattern. Here's why:

1. Budgets vary with the size family. A couple with five chil-dren will spend more for food and clothing, while a childless couple spends more for taxes and entertainment.

2. Budgets vary with the age of the family members. Younger families spend more on children's clothing and doctor bills, while older families spend more on furniture and college bills. Retired people may spend more on travel, medical ex-penses, and domestic help.

3. Budgets vary with where you live. Living costs are higher in cities than in rural areas and small towns, and in the North, East, and far West. On the other hand, incomes are higher there too.

4. Budgets vary with personal interests. Some people like vacations in luxury hotels, others prefer modest camping. One

family may be satisfied with used automobiles, while another insists on buying a new model every year.

5. Budgets vary with incomes. Some expenses are fixed, but others escalate, as one has more for travel, savings, home furnishings, and the like.

6. Budgets vary with climate. Persons living in the South will spend less for winter clothing and utilities than those in colder states. Persons living in the South may spend more for air conditioning in the summer.

7. Budgets vary with temperaments. Impulsive spenders may dribble their money on trinkets, while cautious spenders look for quality merchandise.

8. Budgets vary with regularity of income. Families on set salaries can plan their spending better than those with seasonal income.

*There's a difference in buying a product and being "sold"
one.* This principle is often overlooked. I doubt if one consumer in ten is aware of it.

When I was a young seminarian, with a wife and baby and school expenses to provide for, I was wakened from an afternoon nap by an encyclopedia salesman. I didn't want an encyclopedia, wasn't in the market for one, and didn't have the money for one.

But whether I was half-asleep or whatever, I was "sold" a set, almost against my will! It would have been better had I decided I needed an encyclopedia, then shopped for the best buy!

I have a friend who was an immediate success as an insurance agent. The next thing I knew, he quit. "The company put the pressure on me to push policies on people I knew didn't need them or couldn't afford them, and my conscience wouldn't let me," he explained.

Don't get me wrong. I'm not against insurance people. But there's a difference in the consumer going out in the marketplace and comparing prices and policies and sitting at home waiting for an aggressive salesman to "sell" him something he may not need or can't afford.

I once knew a successful home builder who put a cedar-lined closet in each new house. "The cedar won't keep out the moths, but the ladies love the look and smell of cedar. I've sold more than one house on the basis of the closet," he confided in me.

How often have we made poor buys because of an impulsive decision ("I just love the view from the kitchen window") or because of a persuasive sales person who was more concerned with his commission than our needs?

Everyone needs a little fun money. However judicious a family may be in its spending, each member should have a little fun money to use as he pleases. He shouldn't need to account for it to anyone. What is one person's "waste" is another's pleasure.

A money diary holds many surprises. If you want the surprise of your life, keep a money diary for a month. Put down every dime you put in a parking meter, every quarter you spend on stamps, every half-dollar, or whatever, on a cup of coffee. Anyone with serious money worries should try a money diary. Like the time diary I suggested earlier, it will show how much money gets frittered away.

Whether a money diary works, I don't know, as I've never tried it. I got the idea from various money guides. Like a dripping faucet that wastes hundreds of gallons of water between meter readings, so a dripping purse can waste sizable amounts of money in a year's time. The problem in a family is enlisting cooperation. It's no small chore to keep such a diary.

Enough for the principles. Now for some basics. I'm not going to propose a budget guide or give a long list of money-saving tips. All kinds of literature is available for that. I want to summarize what I call "key words."

As I've said, the careful spender is not out to find the cheapest bargain. Rather, he's out for quality, prudence, and a sense of satisfaction.

Keeping certain key words in mind helps make this possible. Here's what I mean:

THE FOOD DOLLAR: *Nutrition.* Food takes a hunk out of any budget. How does the shopper know a good buy at the supermarket? To me, the key word is *nutrition.* The goal is to feed ourselves not only economically but also well. Vitamins are best bought on the grocery shelf, not at the drug store. Regardless of the skill of the shopper as a bargain hunter, nothing is gained if the family diet lacks the basic foods.

THE SHELTER DOLLAR: *Convenience and security.* Money is well spent on housing if it's convenient to what interests us. What interests us may include schools, shopping, churches, recreation, or places of employment. With the growth of crime in America, *security* is rapidly becoming another key word in the housing dollar. A "bargain" in real estate is no bargain if it forces me to live a long way from my chief interests. This will grow in importance as the cost of cars and gasoline increases.

THE HEALTH DOLLAR: *Prevention.* The patient who sees a doctor or dentist only when he is ill or has a toothache is a poor manager of his health dollar. It's much cheaper to spend money on staying healthy, than trying to restore health. Unfortunately, many families simply don't have the money for preventive medicine.

THE FUN DOLLAR: *Recreation.* Whatever rejuvenates and renews us in a wholesome way, both physically and emotionally, is a good buy for our fun dollars.

THE SECURITY DOLLAR: Peace of mind. We insure our lives, health, and property against the unexpected (illness, accidents, death, storms, and fires). A chief purpose is peace of mind. For example, I hope I never collect any of the premiums I've paid for fire insurance. Yet it's good to know that if an emergency arose, we have insurance or savings to fall back on.

THE CLOTHING DOLLAR: *Self-confidence.* On the practical side, good clothing helps us keep cool or warm, protects us from wind and rain, and makes us presentable and attractive. To me, the key word is *self-confidence.* If my clothing helps me feel poised instead of self-conscious, I'm spending wisely. Dressing too shabbily or flamboyantly may have the opposite effect. I like William Shakespeare's advice in *Hamlet:*

> Costly thy habit as thy purse can buy,
> But not express'd in fancy; rich, not gaudy;
> For the apparel oft proclaims the man.

THE TRANSPORTATION DOLLAR: *Dependability.* How dependent one is on transportation, say, for his work, the more logical it is to spend what's necessary. But if one uses a car only for short, personal driving, there's less need to invest in late models. The person who has the time and ability to tinker around with motors may spend very little for a car.

THE BENEVOLENT DOLLAR: *Christian compassion.* Any spending plan should include generous amounts for giving. And the key words are *Christian compassion* not such cold words as *duty, dues, responsibility, "my part,"* and the like. For one thing, liberality saves us from greed. "Three Arshins of Land," a short story by Russian novelist Leo Tolstoi, tells of an ambitious fellow promised all the land he could encircle on foot in a day. However, if he failed to return by sundown, he forfeited everything. The fellow walked further and further, before circling around to return. Overextending himself, he rushed breathlessly to the starting point, just at sundown. However, he died of exertion, and in the end, got only three arshins of land, the Russian equivalent of "six feet of dirt," enough to bury him in. The application is obvious.

One of my favorite Bible verses is Job 29:15-16, "I was eyes to the blind, and feet was I to the lame. I was a father to the poor: and the cause which I knew not I searched out." It's one thing to be pressured to give, to be promised a place on a roll of honor or public monument. It's another to seek "the cause we know not," to give because of the overflow of our hearts.

A generation ago, Elsie Stapleton, a budget counselor, made a study of two hundred families who gave away at least one-tenth of their incomes. Each of those tithing families impressed her, for never did she find even one in the red. They budgeted their money sensibly. She was impressed with how well-adjusted they were financially, as well as spiritually. "They knew the value of money," she concluded, "and they spent their earnings on what was most important to them. The 10 percent tithe was the most vital of their outlays." My observation as a minister tells me this continues to be true among tithing families, although I would not encourage tithing simply on the basis that "your money will go further."[2]

THE FINAL DOLLAR: *Consideration.* Why do so many people put off writing a will or setting up a trust? Partly from ignorance. Some don't stop to think that if they die without specifing how their property is to be divided the state will step in to decide for them.

For example, in Illinois where I live, if a young father dies and leaves no will, half of his property goes to his children and half to his wife. Would a thinking person want to risk the possibility of the courts naming a guardian for his children to look after their share of the property, when the wife needs it all for herself and her family?

Another reason people don't make wills is that many of us hesitate to face our own mortality. We fear that if we start talking about a will others might think we have a premonition of dying or that we have some secret illness.

Some people put off making wills because they distrust attorneys and banking institutions. Not wishing to "trust lawyers," they try to be their own lawyers. There's a similarity here to the patient who tries to be his own doctor and winds up with a fool for a patient. Likewise, the client who tries to be his own attorney ends up with a fool for a client.

The mistaken notion that estate planning is only for the wealthy and the elderly keep some people from making wills. Actually, the younger a person is and the more modest his resources, the greater the need for professional advice, to make sure what one does leave is well-managed.

I'm aware that I've hit only the high points. Libraries have books and pamphlets galore on every aspect of personal finance. If I have pointed you in helpful directions, I have succceeded.

Still, most of what we learn comes from experience. I've heard the expression, "The trouble with life is you get the grade first and the lesson later." Unfortunately, the same applies to money management.

Here's a little test to help you grade yourself. In each category, select the statement that best fits you. The sentence printed first is positive, while the sentence in parentheses is negative:

1. I look on money as a servant to work for me. (I consider money a god, and I'm willing to be its slave.)

2. I keep discretionary power over some of my income. (Everything I make is spent before I get it.)

3. Saving money is just one of my goals. (I save every possible dollar.)

4. I realize that price is one of several factors in smart shopping. (I always buy the cheapest product.)

5. I allow other members of my family to help decide our spending and saving patterns. (I make all the decisions involving money.)

6. I try to balance needs and wants. (If I see something I want, I buy it, one way or another.)

7. I have friends on several economic levels. (I feel shy and ill at ease around anyone who makes more than I do.)

8. I try to be generous. (I feel other people should get out and work for what they need.)

9. I have a plan for distributing my property at my death. (So long as I get what I want, I can't be bothered about what might happen tomorrow.)

Notes

1. George S. Clason, *The Richest Man in Babylon* (Denver: The Clason Publishing Co., 1930).

2. Elsie Stapleton, *Spending for Happiness* (New York: Prentice Hall, 1949).

9
When You Want To Be Sure

Anytime we bring certainty and confidence to our lives, we are helping ourselves. "Guesstimating" is never the route to poise and self-assurance. We'd like to be certain that every decision we make is correct. But assuredly, that's a dream of the wildest magnitude.

For professing Christians, there are two areas where all of us long for certainty: the assurance of our personal salvation and the rightness of our vocation.

In my ministry, seldom have I met a believer who did not admit a struggle with doubt at one time or another in his life. With some Christians, the doubts are casual and short-lived. With others, the struggle with doubt seems a life-long battles.

I was ten when I accepted Christ as my Saviour. A few weeks later, I was baptized. I had thought about the decision for months, so it was not a snap judgment. Neither was I the victim of religious emotionalism that sometimes sweeps children into premature decisions.

At the age of fourteen, I felt a strong commitment to the ministry and shared this vocational dream with my pastor, George L. Johnson, at the First Baptist Church in Marion, Illinois. He encouraged me without pushing me or sensationalizing my youth.

When I was about sixteen, a friend of mine, Don Bethel, went forward during an invitation to admit that he had made a mistake. He said his earlier profession of faith was not genuine, but he was now ready to make a valid confession.

I admired Don. He was older than I. His father was a Sunday School teacher. His brothers and sisters were more regular churchgoers than my family. So I concluded that if he had been mistaken about his conversion as a small boy, then I probably had made the same mistake.

There was really no basis for me feeling that way, yet the fear claimed a foothold in my mind, and the doubts multiplied. But I kept silent. I couldn't bring myself to tell anyone.

When I was eighteen and a freshman at Southern Illinois University at Carbondale, the Crenshaw Baptist Church, between Marion and Herrin, called me as their student pastor. The small, one-room church was located at Crenshaw Crossing, so named because it was once a stop or "crossing" on an interurban trolley that connected Marion, Herrin, and Carterville. I preached there twice a month. In a few months, the Crenshaw Church requested my ordination, which was set for February 7, 1943.

I approached my ordination with misgivings, for I was still haunted by those illusive doubts that I was a Christian in name only. Frequently, after delivering a sermon at the Crenshaw Church and giving a public invitation, I had an inner feeling that I needed to respond to my own invitation. This made me feel like a hypocrite—a young minister asking for ordination who wasn't even sure he was a believer himself!

In my struggles for assurance, I often prayed, "If I'd never known Christ in a personal way, I do now take him as my Saviour and repent of my sins." But such praying did no good.

I remember the Sunday afternoon when I re-read the great eighth chapter of Paul's letter to the Romans: "There is therefore no condemnation to them which are in Christ Jesus. . . ." I thrilled at the closing verses of that chapter, "Who shall separate us from the love of Christ? shall tribulation, or distress. . . . Nay, in all these things we are more than conquerors."

But I was no conqueror. I accepted the principle of salvation by grace through faith, a faith which is not the result of our good works. Although I saw it with my mind, I could not feel it in my soul.

Southern Baptists make no educational nor age requirements for ordination. The reason is that we believe if a person is confident God has called him to preach, who is man to refuse ordination? And although this sometimes results in abuses, it avoids the larger abuse of denying the pulpit to those who may be lacking in formal education but are rich in experience and sincere in their calling.

If I had it to do over, I would have delayed ordination until I was more mature. On the other hand, my ordination solved my doubt problem about my conversion. So in that sense, it was timely.

Here's how it happened. I spent the weekend of my ordination with my parents at 1404 North State in Marion. After Sunday dinner, I went into the living room and stretched out on the wine-colored sofa with mohair cushions. I closed my eyes and breathed this prayer:

> My precious Lord, in a few minutes, the ordination council will be asking me to describe my conversion experience. You know how often I've prayed for assurance, how I've struggled to make a full surrender to you. If there's anything else to do, I don't know what it is. All I can do is say I have trusted you, and if that's a lie, so be it.

At the two o'clock service, sure enough, the first question was to relate my conversion experience. I described the Sunday morning in that same church, eight years earlier, when I trusted Jesus. I didn't embellish the story, minimize it, or interject my doubts.

The amazing thing is that as I finished my short testimony, all the doubts I'd ever had just melted. I felt the sweetest assurance and have until this day.

Was I "saved" that afternoon when I shared my experience? No. I'd been a genuine believer since I was ten. It just took me that long to accept the truth that God does the saving, irrespective of how we may or may not feel about it. I sensed for the first time that it's faith that saves, not feelings. And regardless of how one "feels," it's impossible to trust Christ and be lost at the same time.

Growing up, I'd heard Dad tell about an uncle of his by the name of Pratus. "Each summer when I was a boy, we had a brush-arbor revival out at Pittsburg east of Marion," he explained. "We knew that on the first night of every revival, there'd be at least one mourner down on his knees at the straw-filled altar. And that would be Uncle Pratus, who'd stay as long as anyone would pray over and for him."

Finally, after several summer revivals, Uncle Pratus "made it through" and claimed conversion. But once he gained assurance, he testified, "You know, all that going forward and praying and begging God wasn't necessary. It just took me that long to turn loose and let God do his work."

In the matter of assurance, we help ourselves best by not helping ourselves. I'm convinced that the people who have the most trouble with the certainty of their salvation are those who are trying hard to do it all themselves. There are those who say that such assurance is impossible, that a person never truly "knows" in this life whether he's saved. If salvation depended on my self-righteousness, that would be true. We'd need to wait for the final judgment to see if we had accumulated more good marks than bad ones!

Some hesitate to claim assurance, lest they appear to boast. True, claiming that one knows he is a saved believer is bragging; but it's boasting on the saving and keeping power of God, not on personal accomplishments.

This is the meaning of 2 Timothy 1:12: "For I know whom I have believed, and am persuaded that he is able to keep that which I have committed unto him against that day." The question is not whether I'm able to "hold out." The issue is faith in a God who is able to hold out for me. Thus, the boasting is in God and is therefore, justifiable.

Some folk "hope" they'll be saved. Others "think" they are, "wish" they were, or "guess" they are. The Bible teaches that we can know.

In fact, 1 John was written for that purpose. Note 1 John 5:13, "These things have I written unto you that believe on the name of the Son of God; that ye may *know* that ye have eternal life" (Author's italics).

A second problem that bothers most people, at some time in life, is doubt as to the rightness of vocational choice. Would I be happier doing something else? Am I really cut out for this job? Should I change vocations in mid-life?

When I was ordained at the age of eighteen, I had no doubt that God wanted me to be a pastor. I never gave it a second thought that I would ever do anything else. I did not foresee the years I would spend working for a denominational body, or editing a Baptist state paper.

I was not born into this tradition. Dad held a number of jobs in his lifetime. He made no decision to enter any one job market. Thus he never served as an apprentice, enrolled in a trade school, or attended college. He didn't even attend high school.

In my father's case, his vocation was a matter of finding whatever job he could. So long as he had a paycheck coming in, I doubt if he spent much energy wondering, "Did I make the right choice?"

Dad worked as a miner, house painter, paper hanger, day laborer, truck farmer, and door-to-door salesman. He also found work in a powder company that made explosives for the coal mines and in the car shops of the Illinois Central Railroad.

Most of his life, Dad was employed within a few miles of his birthplace. As a teenager, about 1899, he sought his fortune in the city of Saint Louis, about 120 miles from his home. Arriving empty handed and with no job prospects, he spent one night in the city jail, not as a prisoner, but because he was friendless and penniless. He walked much of the way home, following the railroad tracks. One night a section crew befriended him, sharing their supper and bedding.

It was his last effort to find "success" outside of a willingness to take nearly any local job that presented itself. He made no professional or vocational choice as such.

Many people who follow this pattern live productive, well-rounded lives. We may categorize them as "common people," but it's the labor of the so-called common people who contribute much to our high standard of living in America.

But people, like myself, who early make a lifetime vocational choice, are concerned not only with the steadiness of a paycheck but also an inner feeling of rightness, a desire for certainty, an assurance that we are "in the right place, at the right time, doing the right thing."

I have no pat answer for those who question the jobs they're now holding, who wonder how they can be sure they should stay, or move, or even shift careers.

I can tell how I've coped with this nagging question. As I said, I had no desire other than to be a pastor, preferably in the same church for a lifetime. Maybe it was a boyish dream, but the dream was real.

Both as a college student and a seminarian, I served churches on weekends and summer vacations for a total of eight years. After graduation, the University Baptist Church in Carbondale, Illinois, called me as its pastor. I served five years, from 1950 to 1955.

Then an opportunity came to do stewardship and church finance promotion for the Southern Baptist Executive Committee in Nashville, Tennessee. I took the job, leaving the pulpit for the denomination. After five years in Nashville, I did similar work for the Kentucky Baptist Convention in Middletown, Kentucky, for another five years. In 1965, the University Baptist Church invited me to return to Illinois for a second stint as their pastor.

I was glad to be back in the role of a pastor, although I was not prepared for the changes that had taken place both in me and in the congregation in the intervening ten years. I stayed in that pulpit only eighteen months, leaving it to become editor of *The Illinois Baptist*.

Minister's talk much about God's will, and I believe in God's will and have made it a lifelong quest. However, I think a person would be claiming near perfection to say that he had always done God's will. To me, God's will is a beckoning goal, a lifetime quest.

As I review my ministry, I feel I should never have left the pastorate for denominational service. I'd better qualify that by saying that if I had known then what I know now, I would have stayed in the pulpit. By "what I know" I mean a fuller picture of the real values in life, plus a larger measure of self-understanding.

The catch is, I couldn't possibly "know" many of those things since I had not experienced them. The best knowledge is experiencial.

So for me or anyone else to say, "If I'd known then what I know now," is to claim something beyond the realm of human possibility. So many of our decisions are leaps in the dark, for which we have no prior experience. We best not clobber ourselves over the head about what we should or could have done. If we are satisfied that we did the best we could, I think we are justified in concluding that we did "the right thing."

Life can be lived neither in a rearview mirror in which we are preoccupied with the past, nor in a telescope in which we are fascinated by the future. So, for me, the only remaining question is, Am I doing the best I know right now, this very day? If so, I can claim "sureness" or "certainty" about my present role.

I like to think of God's will as a long hallway, with a series of doors, opening and closing. We cannot see the entire length of the hallway. What we can see is the distance to the next door. So we open the door at hand, walk a few steps, then open another door.

I enjoy reading Ezra 3:12-13, "Many of the older priests, Levites, and heads of clans had seen the first Temple, and as they watched the foundation of this Temple being laid, they cried and wailed. But the others who were there shouted for joy. No one could distinguish between the joyful shouts and the crying, because the noise they made was so loud that it could be heard for miles" (TEV).

This passage describes the return of Jewish exiles to Jerusalem after fifty years in bondage to the Babylonians. They were laying the foundation for a new Temple to replace the one destroyed by Nebuchadnezzar. Some of the older people, who remembered the glories of the earlier Temple, broke out crying. The younger people, overjoyed at the prospect of their own Temple for the first time, shouted. But the result was confusion: the wailing and the laughter mingled in such a way that no one could tell the difference. I doubt if those who were crying or laughing did much of the actual work of laying the huge foundation stones.

Likewise, preoccupation with the past (whether glorious or disastrous) or fascination with the future (however promising), can never bring the "sureness" that what I'm now doing is right. Life must be lived as we go along. God's will is a living, present reality. His will is never totally bound up in memories of yesterday or dreams of tomorrow. Whatever your vocational choice, you can best help yourself to sureness and certainty by focusing on how you relate to your job today.

While working on this manuscript, I interviewed Joe Bob Pierce, an Illinois minister who changed careers at the age of fifty.

Pierce was a former pastor of the First Baptist Church in Carterville, Illinois, and a former president of the Illinois Baptist State Association. At the time of the interview, Pierce was a projects assistant for US Congressman Paul Simon of Illinois.

I want to share part of the interview to show how one individual coped with uncertainty in his vocation. I quote from it as an example of how one person came to the conclusion that what he does about a problem today is what really counts in solving that problem.

Robert J. Hastings: How did your friends react?

Joe Bob Pierce: Most of the laity were puzzled; they just couldn't understand my changing jobs after 18 years in the ministry. However, some showed strong support.

Q. What about other ministers?

A. Reaction was mixed. Some were supportive, assuring me our friendship wasn't based on my continuing in the ministry. Others were not. Oh, I don't mean they said so eyeball-to-eyeball, but in more subtle ways they inferred, "Oh, I'm not sure I could ever do that." Or, "I'm not sure a preacher could ever be anything but a pastor." Surprisingly, some whom I categorize as more "conservative" were the most supportive. And some whom I think of as more "liberal" were critical.

Q. Did any say they had considered such a move?

A. Again I was surprised, for I'm guessing one out of four said they "wished they could" or "had given it serious thought." Of course, the idea's faced everyone at one time or another. But it bothers me that so few of those who really feel they should change careers don't go ahead and do it. It bothers me that they feel so locked in.

Q. Did you have misgivings about resigning your church?

A. Two things worried me. First, that I might lose everything, materially. Second, public opinion—what would others think? I resolved the first by recognizing that in this life, we eventually lose everything, regardless. As to public opinion, I concluded that if a thing's right for me, that's what I should do.

Q. When did you first think about a change?

A. I think it all started with the sudden death of Bill Harkins, a deacon at Carterville. We were the same age and very close. His death made me more conscious of my own age and where I was going in life. Dad died in February of 1979 and, as my own children grew up and were leaving home, I faced the "empty nest" syndrome. I knew they weren't coming back. So I fell into deep depression.

Q. Did you try to get help?

A. Not at first. I just buried it. You see, I bluster a lot and try to mark my feelings anyway. Oh, I could still visit and mingle in the community. But it was a chore to go to the church office, to do any planning. So I saw my doctor and he checked me out physically, to see if that was the cause. He then put me on medication, but it upset me, and both of us sensed my problem was emotional, not physical. We talked a lot. He said a career shift might help.

Q. Do you still do some preaching?

A. I've done some supply preaching and I've turned down some invitations. Actually, I may be a pastor again someday. But I wouldn't be content as a supply preacher all the time. It's not satisfying enough.

Q. Did you get over your depression?

A. Yes. In fact, I got better as soon as I confided to my wife, Jo Alice, that I could no longer function as a pastor and that I would resign by July 1. And the day I resigned, the depression left me completely. Actually, Carterville was progressive in spirit; the members allowed me to be my own boss; they paid me well. But it got to where they were leading me, and I knew it, and I sensed that couldn't go on. Any congregation needs a leader in the pulpit, not a follower.

Q. Did you know you had another job?

A. No, I resigned not knowing what I'd do. I didn't know where I should be, but I knew I shouldn't be here, in Carterville. To be honest with myself, with God, and my people, I had to go, regardless of the future. After I resigned, I signed up with electrical union 702 in West Frankfort, since I'm a licensed electrician. I thought of moving to Missouri. Then Paul Simon offered me this job. He'd mentioned it earlier, but there was no firm offer.

Q. Since depression strikes everyone, at one time or another, what's your advice when it hits?

A. First, get a good physical exam to make sure the problem isn't physical. Second, be honest with yourself. Trust in God's will, knowing he loves you. Remember, God isn't a warden who wants to keep you locked into the pulpit (or any job), if that's not what you like. I do believe the call to preach is a unique call. That is, I don't think God calls doctors or project assistants like he calls ministers. However, I've never been impressed with ministers who say God "made" them preach. I know I don't want to listen to a preacher who deep inside had rather be doing something else. A minister is to preach deliverance to the captives; he can't do this if he's a "captive" himself, chained to the pulpit.

Q. Are you saying a person should quit his job, preaching, or whatever, if he's dissatisfied?

A. Oh, no. Temporary restlessness comes to everyone. All I'm saying is that, when God called me to preach, he didn't lock me in with no possibility of ever changing! I had 17½ great years in the ministry, followed by a rotten half-year. But I never felt from the start that God "made" me preach or that he would ever force me to keep on. Preaching was always a joy to me. But when it became a chore, I felt God had something else.[1]

Note

1. Robert J. Hastings, "An Interview with Joe Bob Pierce," *The Illinois Baptist*, January 7, 1981, p. 4.

Epilogue

Warren Hultgren, prominent Tulsa, Oklahoma, pastor, talks informally to his radio audience during the offertory on Sunday mornings. It's a personal, chatty interlude in which he relates directly to his listeners.

One morning he told the radio audience a story which a friend had related. It concerned a layman in Tulsa who attended another church, but preferred Hultgren's sermons. The man had gotten into the habit of taking his transistor radio and tuning in Hultgren, while appearing to listen to his own pastor!

It so happened that the man in question heard his own "story" on his transistor radio. In fact, he got so caught up that he stood in the middle of his own pastor's sermon, crying, "Hey, he's talking about me!"

If this book has helped you to see yourself, to mirror your own problems, I have succeeded. For once we see our problems, we are nearer to solving them.

No one has it altogether, regardless of how talented, popular, or successful he may appear. Oh, I know the Sominex ads on television describe a place "where the air is always pure, everyone tells the truth and works hard, and nearly everyone sleeps well at night." But such idyllic places exist only in the fertile minds of ad writers.

Shakespeare wrote that trouble sometimes comes as "single spies" and other times in battalions. Morton's Salt reminds us that

"When it rains it pours." But whether serially or in clusters, trouble knocks at every door.

Life is much like a boat. Whether it's a mighty battleship anchored in the bay or a skiff tied to the riverbank, any vessel in water has one thing in common: It's in constant motion. So life is in constant motion. Some nights, the breakers roar. Some mornings, the ripples merely murmer. But there's always motion, always tension, always trouble of one kind or another.

I hope this book has helped you to single out your problems, and resolve to do something about them. Or, if your problems are overwhelming, that you will not be too proud to seek professional help. What I've written is just a start. But remember that it *is* a start, and the person who starts, however slow or faltering, is superior to him who sits and mopes.

Four wooden steps led up the front porch of my boyhood home. The steps were made of 2 x 4s, nailed to risers. The 2 x 4s were spaced an inch or so apart, so melting snow and rainwater ran off easily, rather than standing and causing them to rot.

Every three or four summers, one or two of the planks would rot out. Unless replaced, the weakened step might give way and cause someone to fall. So Dad took hammer and saw and nailed a new 2 x 4 in place. We could have gone around to the back door, or we could have jumped (or let someone pull us) over the broken step.

Personal problems resemble broken steps. We can avoid them by going around. We can wish for a miracle, hoping someone will take hold and lift us up over the broken steps, or we can help ourselves.

I sense that many people today are sitting around wating for a miracle to fix the broken steps in their lives. I believe God can do anything he wants to, anytime he wants to. I believe in some of the "success" stories in books and TV testimonies in which a person tells how he was "delivered" from this or that.

Some of this is genuine, and some of it is cheap grace, a Madison Avenue exploitation of simple faith. So we see sick people who want good health but who are unwilling to obey the rules of good health. We see reckless drivers who want safety on the highway, at the same time they drive carelessly. We see food and drug-addicted persons who want God to take away the taste for food or the desire for drugs, without any effort on their part.

I guess all of us would like to be youthful and attractive, wealthy and successful, healthy and problem-free, by somehow flying over the broken steps as if we were riding on some magic carpet.

We are often angered when told that part of the solution is in our hands. "That's what God is for," we complain. But to me, it is as great a miracle for God to work through me, using my will-power, my self-determination, my sacrifice, as it is for him to do it all for me.

I wish you Godspeed in first trying to help yourself, before you send out an SOS, either to God, your family, or your best friend.